The
POWER
of
BREATH

The
POWER
of
BREATH

The Gift of Self-Actualization
Through Meditation

MONICA GARCIA DUGGAL

Copyright ©2022 Monica Garcia Duggal

All rights reserved.

Published in association with Per Capita Publishing, a division of Content Capital®.

No part of this book may be reproduced, stored in a retrieval system, or transmitted by any means, electronic, mechanical, photocopying, recording, or otherwise, without written permission from the copyright holder.

Although the author and publisher have made every effort to ensure that the information in this book was correct at press time, the author and publisher do not assume and hereby disclaim any liability to any party for any loss, damage, or disruption caused by errors or omissions, whether such errors or omissions result from negligence, accident, or any other cause.

ISBN 13: 978-1-954020-17-7 (Paperback)
ISBN 13: 978-1-954020-18-4 (Ebook)

Library of Congress Cataloging-in-Publication Data
Names: Duggal, Monica Garcia, author.
Title: The Power of Breath / Monica Garcia Duggal
Description: First Edition | Texas: Per Capita Publishing (2021)
Identifiers: LCCN 2021923356 (print)

14 15 16 17 18 19 10 9 8 7 6 5 4 3 2 1

First Edition

I dedicate this book to Aaron, Katalia, Gabriella, and my mother, Carmen. Thank you for your unwavering love and for always believing in me.

TABLE OF CONTENTS

Introduction..9
Chapter One: My Journey...19
Chapter Two: Pick Your Place..49
Chapter Three: Method..69
Chapter Four: Hormones...101
Chapter Five: Rest and Digest.......................................131
Chapter Six: Clarity..149
Chapter Seven: Why Now?...173
Chapter Eight: Health...201
Chapter Nine: Happiness..221
Chapter Ten: Your Journey..235
Conclusion..263
Acknowledgments...267
Endnotes...269
About The Author..272

INTRODUCTION

"We keep replaying the loops and they in turn, trigger feelings. It's automatic to the point where we believe that we have no choice. But that is far from the truth."

—Kamal Ravikant[1]

"Meditation is an umbrella term that can cover many things. There are purists who think it has to be done in a traditional way, sitting cross-legged and chanting a mantra, but I think there are many routes leading to the same result."

—Dr. Rangan Chatterjee[2]

I started holding my breath when I was four. Maybe I started earlier, but this time sticks out clearly to me. My first meditation as a child started when I was trying to deal with the real pain of two broken bones on my left arm.

It was a nice sunny day in our neighborhood, the birds were chirping, the sun was warm, and I was excited to hang out with my siblings. I was a four-year-old kid hanging out with my older siblings and our neighborhood friends.

A game I would play often with the "big dogs" of our neighborhood in our neighbor's front yard was called "Tarzan." The front yards in our neighborhood were large, with big trees, and the street was very wide and relatively quiet. We used a car parked in the front yard to stand on, and the big tree to tie a rope to. We would get on the car and then jump off, holding the rope while yelling "aahuaaa uaaa uaaaaaaaa!" as we swung. We would eventually stop swinging and land on the ground, or at least this was what was supposed to happen. I was by far the youngest, and being four years old meant my bones and muscles weren't as developed as a six- or eight-year-old's were.

When it was my turn, I was very excited to jump off the car and let out a Tarzan yell, but unfortunately for me, mine was more of a "aahu—" followed by the snap of rope, then an "AHHHHH!" all the way down until I smacked straight into the ground. I remember being disappointed that I did not even get to do a proper Tarzan scream, but that feeling was overshadowed by the severe pain caused by the weight of my whole body landing on my left arm.

My siblings quickly dropped their "big dog" attitude because I was delirious with pain. They looked at me in horror. My parents would surely spank whoever was the oldest of the group, and my oldest sisters did not want to get into trouble. In their panic, they both looked me over and immediately concluded that I was not that hurt. They

INTRODUCTION

told me I merely had a sprain and I would be fine, and they also told me to please not tell Mom, because they would get in trouble. I quickly agreed with their analysis because I didn't want to get them spanked, even as I nursed my clearly broken arm.

They took me to their bedroom and sat on the floor with me. I could not stop crying from the pain, but they were holding me so I could feel some relief. Not even receiving the attention I always craved from them could stop the tears of pain; I was whimpering and they were trying so hard to soothe me. I felt bad for myself, and I also felt bad for both of them. I must have been meditating through my whimpering, because how I was able to sit there, behind the door in their bedroom for three to four hours, was beyond my scope of understanding.

Long story short, my mother went looking for us when we didn't show up for dinner, and not only did my sisters get spanked for keeping me hidden, but I was spanked as well. So there I was, with two broken bones, and I got spanked.

I was sad, scared, and completely pissed off. I was pissed because I listened to my sisters and they still got in trouble, and I also got in big trouble. My mother took me to the hospital and left me there overnight so I could get a cast on my broken arm. I remember that night I dreamt about trying to find my mother. I was also pissed that she left me at the hospital by myself, though I knew she had eight other children she had to go home to take care of. Having sixteen kids is really difficult, but being one of sixteen is difficult as well. As I write and read this now, I realize that anger was how I dealt with my sadness.

I BELIEVE IF I HAD really learned how to meditate as a child, my life would have been so much better.

My current journey started when my sister was hospitalized due to a stroke. I was so relieved to find out she was going to recover; the reality was that deep down inside, I was truly scared and sad, terrified to think that I could have lost her. That was when I bought the book by the British physician and author, Dr. Chatterjee, who wrote an international bestseller about a brave new vision for medicine called *How to Make Disease Disappear.*[3]

My sister had also suffered from other medical problems, and this is why I was a bit overwhelmed that now she had to deal with a stroke on top of her already compromised health history.

During this time I thought it would be good for me to read a book on health and buy one for my sister so she could read it to help her recover. When I reviewed the book, I noticed Dr. Chatterjee's use of breath to relax and meditate, and how easy Dr. Chatterjee made it for his patients to get better.

For my sister, there was hope that learning to breathe would help her learn to relax, which could also help her overall health and recovery from a stroke. The breathing could not only help her get better but could also add years to her life, which I was happy about.

INTRODUCTION

Meditation can help people heal from certain things, like my sister's stroke for example, but for others meditation can simply be a welcome addition for overall improvement.

There are different paths to meditation, to finding peace and happiness through the practice, and also to reaping the health benefits of learning how to meditate and breathe. These simple techniques could literally change one's life for the better.

Maybe you have never truly heard about meditating before or it wasn't the right time in your life when someone mentioned it to you. I recently spoke to some friends about meditation and breathing. They are accomplished and self-aware people, but talking about the subject of breathing and meditation still seems so foreign and boring to them. This simple act of breathing in a certain way baffles people; it appears weird and distracting. I used to be one of those people who scoffed at the possibility of something so simple and free having that much of a positive influence on me.

When you are used to working hard all the time, when you are used to getting lots of things done and putting in effort, tears, and sweat into whatever you're doing, something as simple as taking the time to breathe and meditate seems not only trivial, but also a waste of precious time.

You have to ask yourself: Is brushing your teeth a waste of time? Is sleeping enough hours to be fully rested a waste of time? Is eating a waste of time? Of course not; these are all important self-care practices that make your life better and help you stay a healthy human being.

Something as simple as breathing can seem quite useless on the surface, but I assure you it is not a waste of time. It may not have been on your radar, so therefore, it was truly of no interest to you. However if you are picking up this book (and I am so glad you did!), on some level you are aware of some of the benefits meditation can have for you.

The benefits we get from meditating are huge, from getting to know yourself better, to being able to gain clarity about your world and all the power you hold—the power you have always held. I will show you how meditating can help you be truly happy, help you to find your dreams, and realize them.

The reality is there are dozens—maybe even hundreds—of meditation practices out in the world. Oftentimes, when faced with so much information, we experience a condition known as the Paradox of Choice, where the more choices we are given, the more likely it is we may never choose anything at all or will be easily unsatisfied with whatever we choose. I don't want you to get overwhelmed with the many approaches to meditiation, so instead I will only be covering one: *breathing*. Why? Because I want to make it as simple as possible for you.

Think about it: What is more important than the unconscious, yet undoubtedly necessary life-giving action of breathing? You've been breathing this whole time and most likely haven't thought about it at all! This is why the idea of starting small—focusing on the most fundamental

INTRODUCTION

thing that makes us alive—is a very powerful beginning point and could change your life forever. Breathing can not only calm you but provide energy as well, which I will be detailing in chapter five.

My goal is to impress upon you that anyone can meditate. You can meditate anywhere, at any time, and for any reason. Meditating is free, and you do not need anything at all to do it. You just need to simply decide to do it and then *do* it—nothing more, nothing less. This book is about you finding your path, your way home, your way back to your happiness, back to learning about who you truly are and what makes you happy. Your home is your heart. Sometimes we close our heart, and if you are constantly taking shallow breaths, you can almost be assured your heart is on lockdown, because your whole system is simply trying to survive and get by. You can find more on this subject in chapter nine.

I will be taking you on my journey—a string of events ranging from my childhood, through college, and straight through to the present—all the while revealing through my experience that you too can learn more about yourself and reach self-actualization. Self-actualization is a big idea, but it mostly means that you are discovering yourself and your potential.

You can get connected with your internal voice, just as I did, and reconnect yourself to yourself in order to heal, just as I did. Not only is disconnection a pain in the neck, but it's also a massive energy drain. It is like having a leak in your house, dripping and wasting water for no good reason. Breathing and meditation can help you get rid of those energy leaks and fix the plumbing of your mind, body, and soul, so you can use your energy for what you truly need and want. It is time to fix the energy leak.

The meditation journey throughout my life has taught me to be kind, gentle, and loving with myself by giving myself the space to meditate. When we are kind, gentle, and loving with ourselves, it is like finding the water leak and fixing it. We do not pretend that the water leak does not exist, as we see it when the water bill comes in. What we do is gently find out where the leak is, and then we do the work to patch it up.

This is what meditation does for us: it helps us get to the root of what we need. Rather than pretending that everything is all right when it's not, meditation gives us the grace to deal with it in a real way that will get results. Remember, small leaks can lead to big leaks.

First of all, you must acknowledge the energy drain. Second, you must think of a plan to take care of it. You don't ignore the problem anymore, and you think of proactive ways to fix it. Meditation allows you to have this grace; it allows you to have unconditional self-love while you deal with life.

You may be dealing with a lot of things in your day-to-day world—things that may seem more important than meditating. But you must remember to find a healing path forward. Deep down inside, you know that this too shall pass, and you deal with life. Challenges always come, but because you are giving yourself space to be gentle with

INTRODUCTION

yourself, because you are giving yourself unconditional self-love, nothing can stop you from being happy. Even if there are days that you just want to stay in bed because that is what your body, mind, and soul need, that's fine. There is no shame in taking time to take care of yourself.

You are reading this book because you want to be your happiest, healthiest, and most successful self, and my intent with this book is to start you on your journey to health and happiness using meditation as a form of carving out time for yourself, your future, and for your happiness—*especially* for your happiness.

01
MY JOURNEY

"The bottom line is this: when your energy accumulators stay full, you have more power to accomplish your personal goals, deflect stress, eliminate self-defeating behaviours, and increase awareness. When your accumulators are depleted, life is harder, awareness is numbed, change is hard to make, and you don't feel satisfied (much less happy and fulfilled). Which way would you rather live?"

—Doc Childre and Howard Martin,
with Donna Beech, *HeartMath*[4]

During my childhood I always felt rushed and lost. I felt exhausted as a little kid, not because I was working so hard, but because I always had to be alert. In my home growing up with sixteen children, there was constant stress, and there was nowhere in my home that felt safe enough for me to relax. As an adult, I search for peace and a calm, tranquil environment because I did not have these growing up.

When I was a freshman in high school, I decided I wanted to go to law school. I worked hard in my classes, played sports, and for the most part it was somewhat challenging, but mostly fun. I did not have excessive amounts of stress, as my only job was to get good grades and play sports. When I graduated from high school, I immediately moved to San Diego, California, with my sibling. This was both an exciting and depressing time, since I was leaving my mother and grandfather to be on my own.

When I arrived in California I was ready to go to college, but I learned that I would have to pay more for college if I was an out-of-state student. I did not want to pay out-of-state tuition for college, so I decided I would wait a year and become a California resident. This way I could pay the lower fees. During this impromptu gap year, I felt restless and didn't know what to do while I waited, so I decided I would get my cosmetology license, which took a year to get. This way I could be a hairdresser and pay for some of my school, and this is exactly what I did.

When I finally received my cosmetology license, I got a job at a hair salon by the beach. It was perfect for me, as I was young and I ended up working with a great group of people. I had a great time, but I was still super busy with both work and college—nothing I couldn't handle.

Fast-forward . . . While at San Diego Community College, some of my hairdressing clients were lawyers; we would talk about their work and my goal of becoming an attorney. One of my clients told me that English would be a great undergraduate degree for law school. Another one of my clients told me that UC Berkeley had an excellent

English program, and if I could get my English degree there, that would be a great base for law school.

With all this information, I decided I wanted to go to UC Berkeley and get into the English department. When I talked to my advisor about it, she said I had to play college sports, volunteer, get straight A's, and display other activities that would allow me to be considered for UC Berkeley's English department program.

Once I got the idea in my head, I was determined. I played intercollegiate soccer, I made sure all my instructors knew I had to get A's, and most of my free time was spent in the library, ensuring that I was getting those A's. I volunteered for Read San Diego, which taught adults basic essential reading skills, and I worked full time to pay for my schooling. Now, this became a little stressful, but I had a great support system, and I had tons of fun with everything I was doing, so I was not overwhelmed.

Now, fast-forward again to UC Berkeley, and it all changed. This was now the big leagues. I was no longer a big fish in a small pond; now I was a small fish in the ocean, and I could tell my life would be completely transformed, though how much it would be transformed was still left to be seen. I loved UC Berkeley. I loved my classes. I loved my friends, and I even loved the uphill challenge of competing against the best of the best in the English department.

I had been an avid reader for as long as I could remember. While I was growing up, my grandfather read a paperback book every day, and I had acquired his voracious love of books. He read, so I wanted to read. I remember my grandfather sitting in his rocking chair, reading every single day. I wanted to be just like him, so I had to teach myself how to read.

I would go with my mom to some of the appointments she had downtown. There was one time when I went with her that I remember vividly: I was in the lobby waiting for her, and I remember grabbing one of those newspapers everyone reads and then leaves behind so someone else can read it. For some reason I decided I wanted to read it. I was a four-year-old kid and looked pretty peculiar reading that big newspaper. I had started trying to read it line by line.

I had no idea what I was reading, of course, but I was determined to read it a little bit at a time. I must have been in full concentration mode, because I did not notice when an old man came by me and said, "Hey, do you know what you are reading?" I must have looked not only peculiar but also pretty intense, because he looked amazed. I had to raise my head to take a look at him. I looked up and smiled at him, as he seemed genuinely nice and kind. He smiled and left. I felt a little surprised but mostly determined to continue to read my newspaper that morning in the lobby while I was waiting for my mother. That's when my love of reading really took off. It would be invaluable to me during my time at UC Berkeley. Without my devotion to reading, I would have sunk in the ocean of learning without leaving a single ripple.

PARTLY BECAUSE MY STUDIES were so demanding, my personal journey with meditation began at UC Berkeley in the English department. It was a fun program, but it was extremely challenging, and the competition was fierce, even in the Shakespeare and gender studies classes I took.

In the Shakespeare classes, part of the reason why it was so challenging and very stressful was because many of our topics had all previously been written on by the students who came before us. Shakespeare was the crown jewel of English, and our department was serious about getting novel ideas and papers from every new group of students.

Of course, that was very challenging for many of us. We were told in the beginning of our class that many of us would most definitely receive the very first C's of our lives. When I heard this I remember thinking, *Are you kidding me?* I already knew we were competing for A's, but the way it was presented to us was so stressful. It was as though we were all facing each other in an arena, as if they were saying to us, "We are putting you all in the pit and now you all have to fight for an A. So get ready to fight for your life." This definitely was not what I wanted to hear, especially being a small fish in a big ocean.

We had to think of novel topic ideas for four-hundred year old plays, to come up with something new and creative, to put our own spin on it. Not only that, but we were also supposed to tease the heck out of the idea we wanted to write about. We had to be precise in our definitions and go into great detail, explaining everything in a way that not only made sense but did not bore the reader. The level of detail in defining every single term, and of teasing out our ideas within required parameters, was literally nauseating; it was so much deep, thoughtful work that you would think we were in a PhD program instead of merely getting our bachelor's degrees.

My friend and I quickly learned that our teaching assistants were not going to help us. We had to get the thumbs-up from our professors, and then the real work began. Our writing had to be done in such an intricate way that to just sit down and write something obvious was sure to get you a subpar grade. As a self-proclaimed perfectionist and an honor-roll student in high school at that, I was unsatisfied with subpar grades. This would cause my stress levels to rise to a point I had never felt before and was not prepared to handle.

All the pressure from my college classes was doing a number on me. The stress started getting so bad that I began to get migraines for the first time. I had no idea what those were or how I had started getting them. All I knew was that I started losing my eyesight for a few minutes (characterized by seeing black spots floating around my too-bright vision). This started making my head hurt horribly. Needless to say, the first time I experienced this loss of vision for three to five minutes, followed by the worst pain in my head, was literally debilitating. I pretty much was useless after I got a migraine. The only thing I wanted to do was go to my room, curl up under the sheets, and close off every morsel of light. When you get migraines, any light is bad light; it feels like it is literally squeezing your head together and causing you pain.

As a testament to how I'd lived my life thus far, my first thought was, *This migraine does not coordinate very well with my schedule and deadlines.* Taking time off to deal with this issue seemed impossible. I was living in a co-op by the campus and had a lot of people around me constantly, so it wasn't like I had an abundance of quiet and free time. It was fun, but it was also a bit stressful, as I liked to have my space to study. I got that first migraine, and then it passed. I just wrote it off as a very bad headache, and I did not make much of a correlation between my headache and me losing my eyesight for several minutes before the actual headache. Since I had never experienced anything like a migraine in my life, I did not have anything to compare it to, and my life continued as usual.

Then I got a second migraine. I remember I was working on a deadline for a big paper due in a few days for one of my classes, and the same thing happened—I started losing my eyesight again, the light hurt my eyes, and then I got the brutally painful, intense migraine. I still did not understand what was going on, but I had to get to the bottom of whatever it was. I could barely walk, my head was throbbing so badly, but I thought to myself, *There is no way that I can take the whole day off to deal with this, I need to talk to a doctor.*

The doctor knew what my problem was almost immediately. The doctor gave me some medication for migraines and also gave me a note to let my professors know that I had a medical excuse for the headaches if I ever missed class or deadlines. I still did not think much of my migraines; I remember friends in my co-op telling me to take it easy and to go hang out with them.

I would try to hide away from everyone so that I could focus on my work, as I wanted to get my degree and be happy with the work I put out. Now that I had seen the doctor, I was feeling pretty good about myself. I was feeling as if I was dealing with the problem to take care of my migraines. In my mind, that was that.

But, I was very wrong. I happened to get another migraine, but this time I had some medication. I still had to deal with the very painful headache; though it was slightly muted by the drugs, they did not take care of the actual migraine. For example, the light still bothered me and hurt my head. I still could not see straight or focus on anything, so in essence I could not do my work, as I could not see the writing with blurred vision and a throbbing headache. I couldn't do what I was in college to do.

I went to the doctor again to let them know the medication they gave me did not work very well. I suggested that maybe I needed a different medication, perhaps something a bit stronger. The doctor sent me to a migraine specialist and said I could get something stronger there. I found the office and sat in the waiting room, near another student. We talked about what we were doing there, and I told her I was suffering from migraines. She said she had also been suffering from migraines, and she was there to get even stronger medicine as well; she had been getting migraines for a long time and they had progressively gotten worse. Even with the medication, she could be out for a whole week. After I heard this, I immediately left the doctor's office because I realized taking the medication and getting stronger doses was not going to solve my migraine situation. I felt that the other student who was out for a whole week from her migraine would be my future self, and I had to figure out another plan.

A few days later, a meditation guru was hosting a workshop for students; it was to be held in one of the gyms and was open to anybody. I could not be unable to do my college course work for a week, or I would literally flunk out of college. I was looking for other ways to deal with my migraines, as the stronger medication was no longer an option. I was willing to try new methods to help me find relief from my stress.

I joined the thousands (it seemed like at the time) of students in piling into the large, dimly lit gym for the free yoga meditation class. Many of us were unsure of what would happen next, as we were completely new, not only to the practice, but also to the whole idea of yoga and meditation. There were dozens of rows, and there were small yoga mats on the floor for us. We each found a place to sit. Then the instructor said something shocking: "Some of you are going to cry."

Where is the nearest exit? I thought immediately, *I need to get out of here quickly.* I didn't end up leaving, of course, and not just because I was in the middle of the large gymnasium and there was no way of sneaking out unnoticed. I mean, I was already uncomfortable, having to go to something I had no experience with. And now, the instructor was telling us that some of us would cry, and I did not want to cry; I especially did not want to cry in front of a gym full of other college students. So, I just stood there. But in addition to my discomfort, I was annoyed with the fact that due to my very real problem with headaches, I found myself in this strange room with all these other strange college students, trying to relieve some stress. I started to feel a little sorry for myself for getting the migraines. I was just trying to take my college classes and move on and get a job, for God's sake! How difficult is that?

This line of thinking makes me laugh today because really, is that not what all of us are trying to do? We are not trying to be perfect; we are simply trying to go about life and do our best. We are doing whatever it is that we need to get done, and that is exactly how I felt. I was just trying to get by as a responsible college student, and then I got the darn migraines, and somehow I found myself in that dimly lit gymnasium with a meditation yoga instructor who was telling us we were going to get emotional. First, I am not a crier; I am a fighter. I fight, I pull hair, I bite, I scream, and I growl, but I do not cry. But now all I can do is look back and laugh at my naiveté.

By the time the yoga instructor got the meditation practice underway, I thought it was going rather well. All of my fear of taking this class had abated. I was thinking to myself, *Why all the mental chaos before this class? This is great.* I was beginning to feel very relaxed and actually pretty amazing. Fancy that!

I COULD NOT REMEMBER a time when I had felt so good. I felt completely relaxed and at peace. At that point I had no idea the yoga workshop was going to be so life-changing for me. I was learning that I could make myself relaxed and I could let go for a little while. I did not realize at the time that this meditation yoga practice would take away my migraines forever. This is what my stressed-out self needed. It turned out that while I was busy thinking about the papers I turned in or the papers I would be turning in the future, there was no room for being present and relaxed. The present is where I had control. The past was gone and the future would come, but I could relax and work in the present on the next step I had to take with regard to my papers. When you are a perfectionist, your life exists in the future and the past, not in the present. When you are breathing and doing meditation work, you cannot be in the future and you cannot be in the past; you can only be in the present. Breath is always in the present.

> *When you are a perfectionist, your life exists in the future and the past, not in the present.*

Being such a perfectionist was what kept me living in the past and future; it was messing with my whole being. My nervous system was in a complete knot, and these knots were all over my body. All this stress was what was undoubtedly causing my migraines. The stress manifested itself in those headaches, my brain and body's way of telling me I needed to relax. Our whole body is connected, and I emphasize "whole." A problem does not exist in a vacuum; if there is a problem with one part of our body, it sends a chain reaction through everywhere else.

Okay, let's backtrack a little here . . . How did my migraines start? It all starts in the brain, where our thoughts live. The brain is truly an incredible organ. The brain is like the highway of everything that needs to get done. The thoughts are like the cars. If all lines are open, then the cars go through smoothly, but if there is an accident, or for that matter a bottleneck, then there is a problem. I got a bottleneck from overstress, coming in part from all the papers I had to write. I was trying to deal with everything all at once, and this is how a bottleneck works. In traffic, you have too many cars trying to get through one lane; in our brains, we have too many thoughts, expectations, or deliverables that are trying to get through.

A problem does not exist in a vacuum.

Everything goes into this narrow path, and eventually nothing goes through and everything stops. The road is then backed up and the cars keep coming—in our case, our thoughts. The brain becomes overstimulated and stressed. Nothing is getting through, and the brain has no idea what to do or how to fix it, hence a bottleneck and a mental traffic jam. This causes stress, fight or flight, and the whole system breaks down, which leaves room for the migraines to forcefully shut the overheated system down.

Your brain is constantly trying to repair and create new connections, especially while you're learning new things and growing. This process is called neuroplasticity. Neuroplasticity is where we form habits and forge new skills through practice. If we already have habits that are ingrained in our brains, then these happen without us thinking about them. Some habits stand the test of time with their usefulness, but some don't.

When we meditate, our brain gets a break. It does not have to think about our thoughts or any habits we have. This means that when we meditate we give our brain a much needed rest so that it can find out if what we are thinking and doing is in alignment with what we truly want and need.

Your brain does both the low-level and high-level work; the daily, basic things are the neural pathways you have mastered that do not require much thought, and the high-level work requires more time and attention, and therefore, more energy. For example, a low-level brain job would be a habit, like when you get home and you don't remember driving back. This would be your brain working on autopilot or rather following a very ingrained neural pathway that would take less energy to do.

On the other hand, high-level brain work might be remembering a proposal that is due tomorrow, and this would require much more energy because, on top of your brain having to remember this task, it is also doing low-level work like breathing and yes, driving you home. Your brain is constantly working on something.

The problem for us then can occur when we have too many things to keep track of in our brain. When we think of a computer, we think of the virtual memory capacity it contains, and if only a few windows are open, we are okay. However, what happens if we have tons of windows open? Then everything starts to slow down, and after a while we cannot open any more applications or windows because there is no longer any room. Your brain is already doing tons of work—all of your low-level jobs—and now you start to add one, two, three, or more high-level brain jobs. Like that overheated computer, your system is also going to stop, stall, or break down, resulting in negative physical consequences.

This piling up of open requests to the brain takes up a lot of energy and makes us work much harder than we should. If we are walking around clueless as to what is going on with us, we are doing ourselves a disservice. It is unfortunate that many of us have never learned how to find out what we are thinking and what it is we actually need.

This sounds simplistic; however, it is not. We spend all day every day putting up a façade of being okay. Simply because we look alright on the outside does not mean we are as okay on the inside, and it is our job to ensure that we are okay on the inside. One very simple way to ensure we are doing this is to close all those windows and allow our computer, our brain, to take that much-needed break. With a computer, we may need to just take five minutes to close those forty-plus tabs down, wait another five minutes, and try opening just one or two crucial tabs at a time. The same idea applies to our brains; when we meditate and breathe for five minutes, we can clear all the clutter out and then spend another five minutes figuring out the next one or two items we have to do. We will feel more relaxed, and our brain and body will feel more energized and in alignment.

A little stress—for example, about getting low grades—can actually be okay and healthy, but when that stress becomes obsessive and we cannot turn it off, other health concerns can crop up. When we do not get any relief from too much stress it starts to add up and cause problems.

I have not done research on what other ailments come from stress on the body, as I truly do not care to find out what terrible things can happen from stress. I am sure many people suffer in different ways, and stress can cause some serious health issues for them, but meditating is also a real solution for these people. The ailments that happen from stress are real, and the solution of finding a remedy through breathing and meditating is also very real.

For me, it was the migraines. The other student trying to get more medication for her migraines likely was not dealing with the underlying stressors that were causing her headaches in the first place.

How long can we avoid being clear with ourselves about what we truly need? Considering my perfectionist tendency to do, re-do, and do more work again, it is no wonder I started getting migraines. Not only was I already hard on myself, but suddenly I was in an environment where they wanted us to learn how to be better. It was the perfect storm for me to work even harder than what I had already worked in the past. All of this was tough on me. I did not see any light at the end of the tunnel, and I did not know how to take a break from it all. I had no real tools to deal with the stress I was having in college. I tried to do what I had done all my life, but this time, these skills of persevering and just continuing to move forward were not going as planned. I persevered and felt the consequences, but by learning meditation yoga and breathing, I learned how to persevere with built-in breaks, which made all the difference in the world.

My stress affected my mind, body, and soul, and it stemmed from all the expectations from myself, my professors, the department, and the world. You heard right: I was so caught up in my state of stress, I felt as if the whole world sat on my shoulders. And I paid for it. Logically, I know the whole world is not on my shoulders, and my heart knew that, but my brain did not. This is why our thoughts are so important, because if we tell ourselves the whole world is on our shoulders, then our brain says, *Okay, how do we get the whole world off our shoulders?*

If you are going to work on your goal, you want it to happen, and you make time for it, great. However, if you put a goal in your brain and you do not believe it or you are not that committed to it, it will just add tons of stress to your life, so tell your brain you do not want that goal anymore and to move on.

Contrary to what we may believe, the brain is not logical. It's not exactly like a computer that just takes the code you give it and tries to make it happen. This sounds a bit weird because the brain is so intelligent, but it's actually the heart that makes the brain smart. You have to decode the reasons why certain habits or perpetual thought loops are going round and round in your brain.

The impact these thoughts can have on our whole body's wellbeing sounds ridiculous, but if we think about the power of our brain, it is not ridiculous at all. I have conversations with all sorts of people, from all ages and walks of life, and when I talk to them and ask them questions about their thoughts, some of them have no clue what they think about often or constantly, or why they think the way they do. All of it boils down to having real conversations with ourselves and others about things we feel and do, and maybe sometimes talking about what we don't want to talk about.

In one of my UC Berkeley classes, the point of the class was for us to understand the "why" behind the way we think. If we had never exercised these important skills before, UC Berkeley was the perfect place to make us start to think about what we were actually thinking about, our values, and our ideas. They made us question why we felt a certain way about something, *and that is who you are* . . . but why do you feel this way, and where did you get these ideas from?

Bam! There it was: a completely uncomfortable line of thinking. It was the first time many of us were actually challenged to think for ourselves outside of our parents and our cultures. It was eye-opening, because many of us were so clueless. We thought, *This is just the way things are.*

The process made us stronger thinkers. The purpose was not to change our mind, it was simply to say okay, just take ownership of your thoughts and of who you are; be intentional and do not do things because it is easy and habitual, because that easy route of not thinking about who you actually are and what you need becomes the hard route down the line.

Even though some of us are gifted and privileged to have learned these skills, many of us do not understand that we have the power to make our own decisions and live in a higher, happier state of being.

Kathryn Hansen, an author who suffered from several health issues, wrote a book called *Brain over Binge*.[5] What I loved about her book was that it was completely raw, meaning it was such a beautiful book about her process of learning self-awareness. She struggled with all these expectations that she put on herself, which started when she was a teenager.

When we are at that age, there is a lot of turmoil within us; our brains and bodies are changing, our ideas and our executive functions are developing. That is a whole lot for one person to go through. Even if an individual is in a very supportive and loving household, these years are challenging. Do you remember when we discussed earlier about the brain being like a highway, with our thoughts being the cars? Well, teenage years are like a bottleneck on the freeway, and it's what teenagers have to deal with day after day, so let's give them a break.

Couple all that growth and change in the teenager's

brain and body with all the misguided messages from the external world, and what you have is a disaster waiting to happen. For example, Hansen talks about how if she just could have listened to herself, she would have avoided all of these health issues and the years she spent trying to seek professional help. This could be the challenge about getting information from outside of ourselves: we start to go down a road that may not benefit us, and as in Kathryn's case, we cause ourselves hardship and grief. When we start to compare our insides to other peoples' outsides, we run into trouble.

Kathryn sought the help of many professionals because she had to get better; she was fighting for her health. She went to many psychiatrists and psychologists but was unable to get the help she needed. She finally learned from someone to just tell her lower brain "no" when she had the urge to indulge in her unhealthy habit. She was able to make a new habit of saying "yes" to her health, and "no" to her lower brain's unhealthy requests. If you read her book, you will see that I have simplified her story a lot here, but the fact remains that we always know what we need if we breathe and take the time to listen to ourselves, canceling out all the noise around us. In this way, we can get what we need for ourselves and our health.

Struggle 101: this is when your brain or logical mind says one thing and your body, or what Hansen calls your lower brain, says something else. My take on how she explains it in her book is that she believes we all have the higher brain, which knows what we truly need, and then we have a lower, animalistic brain. In Hansen's case, the difficulties began when she was a teenager and started getting influenced by what she was hearing from her peers and environment about eating habits. She started to question her own eating habits, thinking she might not be eating correctly somehow. She started stepping away from what she intrinsically needed, which was to continue to run and eat like a normal teenager. Because she started hearing chatter about diets and dieting at an impressionable age, she started thinking this was something important for her to also consider. Unfortunately, it was a misguided message that many young, healthy women absorb to their harm.

Hansen mentioned that although she struggled with the lower brain, she also saw how it was useful for her survival and thus recognized its value. This is extremely telling of the depth of her work and understanding about her needs. She was able to connect all the pieces together, which goes to show that though we can be a bit confused by the outside world, the answers have been and always will be within us when we are ready to listen to them.

The way I deal with the dichotomy is by pairing the two together. I like to think of unconditional self-love, and this pretty much gets rid of "good guys" and "bad guys" in one person. When we have unconditional self-love, there is only one player, one real human being that is having a real human experience—nothing more and nothing less.

We are people walking around this world, living a real life full of challenges, so wouldn't it make sense to deal with the challenges with grace when they come up, rather than fighting constantly with ourselves all the time? It's not only exhausting, but it's also horrible for our minds and bodies because of all the stress it causes. We cannot aspire to flawless perfection.

Many of us were not fortunate enough to know that we were not supposed to be perfect. We were taught to be superhuman, unstoppable, a flawless person. It is fine to try your best, to show up and be intentional, but perfectionism is an unfortunate ideal that keeps people unhappy. Carol Dweck, a Stanford University professor who wrote the book *Mindset,* discusses the difference between being a perfectionsist and simply learning and growing without having to be perfect.[6] She claims that perfectionists have fixed mindsets that cause much undue stress. On the other hand, a growth mindset allows one to learn new things and actually enjoy the process.

I read this book when I was trying to find out how to give my kids feedback when they did something for school. The idea was if I did not give them a specific example when I praised them or gave positive reinforcement, then they would get a perfectionist message from me and would not want to ruin being perfect by actually trying to learn things. If I only said to them, "great job," they would not know exactly what I was talking about. But if I was specific about what I was reinforcing, then I could say, "Great job *completing all your writing for that chapter,*" or "Great job *finishing packing for the trip.*" Then they knew exactly what they were getting positive recognition for and could easily do it again. In this example, the child can feel good that not only did they pack all their stuff or finish their homework correctly, but they got recognized for their effort and will likely see their actions make a difference in their lives.

To make the idea of perfection even more damaging, we usually do not know what is perfect, because the word on its own is not only unhelpful but is also superficial. When we do this to ourselves, we are trying to fullfill something that does not exist and is impossible.

Well, thanks a lot to whoever put it in my head that I had to be perfect; I could have still reached my goals without having to be such a perfectionist and a migraine sufferer! But I guess I would not be writing this book if I did not have the challenge of being a recovering perfectionist. Meditation gave me the tools to know I am okay with being imperfect.

It was through finally getting relief from my stress that I learned that stress in small doses is okay and is actually very beneficial to us. However, giving ourselves breaks from this stress is imperative and relaxing. When I learned to meditate, it became a new tool in my "life kit." That tool, the gift I could give myself, was to learn how to relax whenever and wherever I chose to do so. This was such an amazing thing for me and for students all over that college campus to learn: we could turn our brains off for a little while, give them a break, and the world wouldn't explode. This practice went a long way in taking the world off my shoulders.

That fateful day in the overcrowded gymnasium, I encountered this tool for the first time. The bulk of the practice started off in pretty standard fashion, and it came after we did our standing meditation arm yoga poses (which are merely learning how to take long deep breaths in and out while lifting your hands to the ceiling in four different reps, for a total of five to seven breaths each). What was fascinating was that when we used our arms, some of us could not breathe out or inhale slowly; we would move our arms very quickly, meaning that our breathing was fast and we could not slow it down. When the instructor noticed many students doing this, she assured us that we would benefit more the slower we breathed in and out. For me personally, I felt like my breathing just did not work that way. Needless to say, even this part of the practice was super hard for me; for one, I had never thought about my breath before in any real way. Who knew breathing was even a thing? I find this comical. Can you believe this young college overachiever, who thought she knew everything, was extremely competitive and good at what she set her mind to, had paid no mind to breathing before?

We could turn our brains off for a little while, give them a break, and the world wouldn't explode.

Obviously, if you do not breathe, you're dead. Has that fact ever crossed your mind? If not, no worries; it had never crossed my mind either. I guess I was doing okay for a long time there—until I had boatloads of stress, which just kept piling on. I had never experienced anything like that in my life because I usually had an outlet, or I could change my thoughts and focus on something else for a while. But that was not enough this time. The migraines were my bottleneck, so my brain finally said, "I've had it, I am done." In retrospect, maybe I wasn't doing alright even before the headaches hit; that was just the point where I connected the dots.

After completing the standing part of the yoga meditation it was time for us to get on the floor. I was feeling okay right about then. I didn't feel anxious, stressed, or wound up in a tight knot. This experience hadn't been a waste of time. We lay on our mats and did things I somewhat recognized, like the child's pose, the dead man's pose, and other things I was completely unfamiliar with. Let this be a lesson to you: when you don't know what you're doing or don't know the correct terms for things, you merely have to look at your mat neighbor and copy them until you have it down. (Believe it or not, I don't always know the name of the yoga poses on the mat, but give me a strategy assignment and I will kill it every time. I am a badass when it comes to strategy, but I am not so good when it comes to the technical terms of yoga.) You should know that you do not have to be an expert in yoga and meditation to appreciate, and most importantly, benefit from meditation.

The crying started when the instructor started giving us visuals. We had our eyes closed, and we were about as relaxed as we'd ever been; I never knew that I could ever feel this relaxed in my life.

The first visualization was the following:

"Be aware, touching and feeling every nerve, muscle, and cell in your toes, and when you breathe out, relax them . . . Be aware, touching and feeling every nerve, muscle, and cell in your legs, and when you breathe out, relax them . . ."

. . . And on to every part of the body including our faces, eyes, and heads. This first set of visualizations was amazing, and we reached a deeper level of relaxation.

Then we went through the second set of visualizations, and I think this is the one that we stressed-out college students felt the most deeply in terms of de-stressing, the one that made some of us get the relaxation tears in our eyes: when the knots in our wound-up college bodies finally unfurled and gave our brains a much-needed break between difficult classes.

The instructor said to us:

"Now we are going to go deeper into your relaxation practice. Imagine you are a very light pile of stardust glistening in the moonlight, and you are lying there very relaxed, warm, happy, healthy and gently on the ground, and a very gentle breeze comes over you, and when this very gentle breeze goes over you, it takes off the topmost part of your stardust, and it is gently blown away from the very top portion of your pile and feels so good. The breeze moves very gently, very slowly, very calmly, and you feel so relaxed, wonderful, and amazing. And now another very gentle breeze comes over you, and it takes off another very thin layer of your uppermost pile of stardust, and it goes off with the breeze very gently, very slowly, and very calmly..."

. . . And the meditation was repeated a few more times.

Crying took on a different meaning then. They were

not tears of pain, but rather the sleepy tears of a person exhausted and ready to go to bed at night: someone who has found relaxation in their whole system, nerves, brain, and soul. Just as a baby or a little child would get a little tear coupled with a nice, healthy yawn, signaling that the child is very tired, has had an amazing day, and is now ready to go to sleep—the tear acts like the body's signal that it has reached a state of relaxation.

I DID NOT GET MASSAGES as a kid, but now that I have gotten therapeutic massages as an adult, I understand the relaxing effects and health benefits it gives a person's body. Massages are good for many things, including post-workout muscle relaxation, helping a person handle daily stress, or just general relaxation after a busy day. Meditation is somewhat like getting a massage, in that it helps with similar needs of the body and mind. It is exceptional because you can do it anywhere and it is free.

That one yoga class was so beneficial to me. I cannot believe that I had wanted to leave the room before the class had even started, that I wanted to be anywhere but there. It was lucky, then, that I could not leave the room. This short meditation yoga class changed my life forever, and this is what I would love to give you: a practice of meditation that does not cost any money, can be done anywhere at any time, and can change your life for the better.

I will continue to remind you that meditation is worth

it. I would like you to build the neurons in your brain with this messaging and then with the actual practice of meditation. I would like you to build a network that is so thick with the idea of meditation as a health benefit that you make it a regular practice in your life. To give yourself the practice of meditation on a regular basis is to give your brain and your whole being a break from stress.

As mentioned before, if we keep up the practice, our brain will go through neuroplasticity, which means it will change and open a channel for us to relax on a regular basis. Think about it this way: a habit, doing something new, takes a little time to learn, but once you learn the skill then it is much easier to do; it becomes part of who you are.

It's also worth thinking about that if you are usually going, and going, and going, and this is your habit. Your brain will not stop you until it is an emergency, for the most part. However, if you learn how to meditate, then you will rewire your neurological networks to become less focused on going and going, to instead allow you to take breaks, breathe, and meditate. You are creating a new habit and new networks, making you a more relaxed and more productive individual. This sounds counter-intuitive, but think about it. Returning to our highway analogy, you can put as many cars on the highway as you like, but that doesn't mean the traffic is going to move. Then you end up not going anywhere, and you're not going to get that much done anyway, if anything at all. Creating these new networks and neurons in your brain to replace the old, outdated, unhealthy habits of pushing yourself without giving yourself breaks helps you avoid that bottleneck.

There is an idea in the world of business: the Rule of Seven.[7] If we hear or see something seven or more times, it becomes something we recognize, part of our world. It is like an affirmation we say over and over to ourselves, until our whole being feels comfortable and even sees meditation as a habit. The habit of meditation, then, will transform us in the same way.

MEDITATION

THIS IS NOT ANOTHER meditation book that is going to confuse you; this is a book on meditation that wants you to learn and incorporate meditation into your life on your terms.

First, I want you to think about the word "MEDITATION." I don't want you to meditate; I only want you to think about the word "MEDITATION" for a little while. There is no right way or wrong way to do this, there is only a curiosity.

I just want you to imagine that you hold the word "MEDITATION" in the palm of your hand. Take the time to look at it and spin it around. Still holding it in the palm of your hand, look at it as a cool gadget that can help you enjoy your life more.

What you are holding in the palm of your hand is powerful. "MEDITATION" is life changing, but it is also simple, fun, accessible, and relevant to each and every individual who wants to use it to help them live a better, more joyful life.

The reason we are merely talking about the word meditation and not doing any actual meditation is because the actual word can take on so much meaning. Take a close and personal look at it so that you can see it with your own eyes, you can feel it with your own feelings, and you can decide how you feel about it outside of anyone else or any expectation of what it should mean to you.

You can create whatever relationship with "MEDITATION" you want, beyond what anyone else has ever thought about it, outside of anyone else's practice. Get in touch with it.

QUESTIONS

- Have you ever wanted to start a journey with meditation or tried and failed to make meditation a habit in your life?
- Did you feel like a scientist in a lab exploring the specimen of "MEDITATION," or did you feel

awkward holding the word in the palm of your hand?
- How do you feel about approaching meditation in this way?

02

PICK YOUR PLACE

"I've honed a selection of breathing exercises that are incredibly easy and quick, and they can deliver a lot of benefits of meditation, such as stress reduction, pain relief, increased focus, and better sleep quality. They can be done almost anywhere, as frequently as you like—unlike other powerful medicines, you can't really overdose on breathing."
—Dr. Rangan Chatterjee, *Feel Better in 5*[8]

In the yoga class at UC Berkeley, I did not make the connection until much later that what actually helped us relax our bodies was the breathing part of the whole exercise. Sure, I understood that breathing was integral to the yoga movements and to the visualizations we did while we were lying down, but I did not truly think that the breath work that we were doing was the key to helping us deal with the stress we were feeling as college students.

When I gradutated from college, I found a great job. It was fun and dynamic, new and exciting. When I would go to work, if there was a big meeting or something particularly important that would make me a bit nervous or overwhelmed, I would just take some time to do my meditation breathing. It was mainly using my arms while slowly breathing, which was what I learned in that college yoga class.

I would find a place at work that was private and relatively peaceful, and I would do my breathing meditation for only five minutes. These five minutes allowed me to relax and be present for what I had to do next. It took me out of my worry mentality and it put me right where I was supposed to be. The five minutes would help me feel confident, happy, and excited about the meeting or other important tasks that were at hand.

The crucial aspect of meditating was that I learned the signals my body would give me to let me know that I was getting a bit stressed out. This would notify me that I needed to take a little time to stop, find a quiet area, and meditate. It was great to finally gain this clarity and self-awareness, as well as avoid stress migraines.

We can literally meditate anywhere. We tend to think that there is a specific place we are "supposed" to do it. By thinking this way, we actually stop ourselves from meditating. If you have thought of meditating or seen examples of someone meditating, it is usually by the sea, a pond, or a gently moving river.

This is great for the people with access to these environments, but trust me, you don't need them to find what you need through meditation. Therefore, it does not matter where you are meditating, you can pick whatever place you want. Some of these places by the water and the gentle rivers are beautiful and calming, and they make the whole experience much more enjoyable, but in order to get all the benefits of meditation, it doesn't matter *where* you do it, but *that* you do it.

Meditation is like brushing your teeth. When I was climbing Mount Kilimanjaro in Tanzania in the summer of 2017, the guides who were helping us climb to the peak would be walking around early in the morning, brushing their teeth—way up on the mountain where we would camp out overnight. It was strange at first; we were roughing it, so why would we care about brushing our teeth out in the wilderness? The answer is simple: because we need healthy teeth for a healthy life. The obvious places to brush our teeth are in the bathrooms in our homes, condos, or apartments, or wherever we live, but I have seen people do it in all sorts of places. People brush their teeth in the airport bathroom and on the plane (you are given a tooth brush to brush your teeth on long flights) or while they are driving their cars (though I don't particularly recommend you do this).

> *In order to get all the benefits of meditation, it doesn't matter where you do it, but that you do it.*

Therefore, if we can brush our teeth practically anywhere, then we can meditate anywhere. It's actually easier, because it's not necessary to have anything special to do your breathing. You are always breathing, so you can take your breath with you everywhere—and meditate.

You can choose a meditation place by a gentle river (if

you have access to one), or in your car, your bedroom, the living room, your backyard, on a nice walk, on a gentle jog . . . you can pick your place anywhere you want. The best part of all of this is that you get the same results wherever you meditate. Your body, mind, and soul will get the same benefits as the renowned meditational yogis and gurus. I know this does not seem possible, but it truly is.

Don't let having a specific place stop you from meditating. We can stop ourselves from meditating because we can't find the perfect spot, but we should remind ourselves that "perfect" does not exist. Just remember: we are always breathing in any place we find ourselves, so we can meditate wherever we are. The place, then, is not a reason to not meditate, because we can breathe anywhere, and therefore, we can meditate anywhere as well.

There is no specific place you must meditate for it to be the most effective. You may find that you want to meditate in your closet because it is the only room in the house that is quiet enough for you to concentrate. You may also find your car is a quiet place to meditate; or maybe a corner of a room in your house has a good, peaceful environment and you want to start your meditation practice there. Some people also like to meditate in their rooms, standing next to their window, sitting on their beds, or in front of their beds on the floor; others like to meditate in the shower as they are getting ready for their day, or meditate right after they are showered and dressed, before they leave their rooms. Or maybe you will find that a nice, short walk, taking you two and a half minutes away from

PICK YOUR PLACE

your home and two and a half minutes back, is the right place for you to meditate.

You can try a different place every time, or if that seems like too much work, you can designate a place for two weeks or a month and try it out to see how it feels. If it works, you can continue to use that space, and if it does not, you can try something new. You are in charge here, and the better you get at feeling secure with picking the place you want to meditate, the closer you will be to enjoying it and its benefits.

Maybe these suggestions gave you some ideas of places that are simple and easy for you to meditate. Like I said, you can try different places or you can pick one place, stick to it, and then change it up later. It is all up to you; this is your practice, this is for you and your growth, happiness, health, and success.

I have meditated just about everywhere. I have meditated in the park, while jogging, in my bed, in my backyard, in my front yard, at work, at a restaurant, at the airport, at a conference. I literally have meditated just about everywhere I've gone. When I feel I want to touch base and bring myself back to the present, I just start thinking about my breath. This automatically alerts my mind and body that I am coming in. It alerts my entire self that I am taking good care of myself.

There is something very special about this messaging; it's as if you have a great friend, or a loving parent, or anyone else who champions you and knows how awesome and amazing you are. It is like having a beautiful, kind,

THE POWER OF BREATH

caring, and loving person reach over and give you a hug. It is that beautiful feeling of love, kindness, and presence that you give yourself every time you meditate.

Can you imagine how nice it is to get this beautiful hug from yourself by just meditating? When I am driving through hectic traffic and I want a little relief from the stress of driving on a busy highway, I usually just start to pay gentle attention to my breath and count to ten. This is not a hard thing to do; all you are doing is paying attention to your breathing and counting it. It's such an easy way to come back to center again and pay attention to yourself.

Even though my meditation while driving is not an intense breathing exercise, simply counting my breath and paying attention to it slows me down and brings me to the present moment. If we allow ourselves to meditate anywhere we choose, then we can fit meditating into our busy lives and not be discouraged by not finding the "perfect" place for our meditation practice.

YOUR BRAIN IS TOO busy to shut itself down because it is always trying to take care of business for you. It works day and night for you, but you know deep down inside that it needs to rest; it needs to shut off for a little while so that it can figuratively breathe.

Your brain, unless you give it a break, will want to be going over what it needs to do next. This is its job, so we can be grateful for that, but we also need to take care of our brain, and when we meditate, it is like we are giving it some fuel, food, and relaxation from whatever it is working on.

When we meditate on a regular basis, it is like we are allowing our brain to go to the gym and spa, all at the same time. In order for the synapses in our brain to form and become strong, we need to allow them to rest. While you might want to find that perfect place to meditate, all your brain wants is to not think for a while.

When we close all the windows and apps on our computer, it has a chance to cool off. So too when we meditate. It is like we are closing all the thoughts and stress the brain is working on and giving it a mental nap. When you come back online, then your brain only has one or maybe two things to deal with and not a jumbled desktop full of things.

If you read meditation books, especially those on more advanced versions of meditating, it can become extremely complex very quickly. The reason is that some of these meditation books want you to go to these elaborate places to meditate, and then they have specific ways in which you would meditate: for example, sitting down with your legs crossed in front of you.

They want you to pick a place under a tree in an open meadow, by the side of a stream, with the birds chirping in the trees. You get the picture. It is no wonder many of us do not meditate, or we get scared off from the practice entirely. Or worse yet, we get overwhelmed and stressed out even more. This negates the whole point of meditating in the first place, which is to make your life easier. It helps you sleep better, it helps you reduce stress that causes migraines, and it helps you with a host of other ailments that your body could create when you are overwhelmed with stress and life in general.

The very serious versions of meditation are beautiful practices, although unfortunately, they do not apply to most of us. Many of us do not have access to what some of the serious meditators have: gentle streams, trees on the slopes of rolling hills, and other beautiful sanctuaries in which to meditate. Most of us are mothers, fathers, brothers, sisters, friends, neighbors, telemarketers. Most of us are just people trying to do our best with what we have, and simply because we do not have access to the "optimal" environment does not mean that we cannot benefit in picking a place—our bedrooms, our bed, our cars, anywhere—and meditating. We get the same result as all of the greats, we get to give our brains a break, we get to release stress, and we get the opportunity to feel absolutely amazing.

Ignore those complicated books. What you should truly be focusing on is just getting started. Begin a meditation practice today. The times I have stopped meditating in the past are when I have done more confusing research on the subject. The crossed-leg position is something I have never been able to do or ever known why I would have to. Should I stop myself from meditating if I do not have access to a specific tree, or pose? This is not a reality for many of us, but just because these things are not available does not mean we cannot benefit from meditation.

The bottom line is that the health benefits of meditating outweigh the idea that you must find the perfect place and that you should do it perfectly. Or, that you must think perfect thoughts to be transported to nirvana. The first thing to do is start a meditation practice; the rest of the meditation learning will come to you naturally. Your body and mind will tell you what you need.

THE MORE YOU MEDITATE, the easier it becomes to find your zone. When we think of meditating, what we're talking about is stopping whatever it is we are doing and becoming present. This means we stop and we breathe for five minutes—or one minute, for that matter. We do not worry about anything that has to do with our breathing meditation work. All we have to remember is that we are doing it and it is good enough. Remember, the more we do it the better we get, so the fact that we are doing it at all is very good for our health, mind, and body.

The more we practice meditation, the easier it will be for us to access our meditation practice. The more we do it, the more we will become familiar with what works best for us and how we like to do our meditation. We stop the train of thoughts that are running through our mind. We gently start to breathe, listening to our breath as we are focused on it. We are meditating now. We breath in and out for one to five minutes.

There is no judgment when we are breathing, there is no right or wrong way to do it. We are just breathing. We get excited and happy that we are in the present focusing on our breathing. This is our meditation practice. Yes, it is that easy. Yes, it is that helpful and healthful. It will help you tremendously. You will be happier when you meditate; you will start experiencing amazing results in situations which brought you much anxiety in the past.

Meditation, like everything else in this world, is another addition to our tool box. We can all do it differently, and the way we do it is for our unique benefit. The main goal is that we follow through with it; the only way to benefit is by actually doing it. We do not get the benefit of a meditation practice by thinking about it or by not doing it because it won't be perfect from the beginning.

The idea of screwing something up is our perfectionism talking, and "perfect" is not real. It does not exist, no matter what anyone says. We are humans, and we learn. We learned how to walk, so we can learn how to meditate.

I LIKE TO BUILD HABITS, and I knew that meditating was not something I wanted to let go of. I decided that I

PICK YOUR PLACE

wanted to approach mediation the same way I do sleep: something that I have to do every day, something that is vital to my health. So I told myself, *Meditation will no longer elude me, meditation will no longer escape from me, meditation is a way for me to practice self-care, a way to keep me happy, healthy, and successful.* I committed to making it part of my life forever, until I am not breathing anymore.

I know this can sound ridiculous, but is it, really? Let's think about it. If you do not take your showers, if you do not brush your teeth, if you do not sleep every night, what is going to happen to your health? Exactly! Bingo! You are not going to be happy. You can pretend that self-care is not important for whatever reason, but you will eventually face the consequences. Life is better when you are taking care of yourself, and meditation is another habit or tool that you need to live a less stressful and happier life.

We are humans, and we learn. We learned how to walk, so we can learn how to meditate.

This is how I determined that I would add meditation into my arsenal of habits as something that was a non-negotiable, just as getting enough sleep is a non-negotiable for me. I can do it anywhere, because wherever I need to meditate is the right place for me.

I always thought hard about creating a space for me to meditate when I traveled so that I would not stop my practice. I had started meditating for twenty minutes every morning. This truly was hard for me because I was ramping up my practice. When I had started meditating again, it was not for my health but to reach my goals and stay focused throughout the day.

Reaching your goals and being healthy can both be achieved by meditating, but the way I looked at meditation was very different each time I picked up the practice. The benefits of meditating are so vast that you can actually pick them up for one purpose and find that they help you with a bunch more.

I was practicing for twenty minutes every morning as soon as I woke up. I would meditate, clear my mind, and relax. This sounds a bit silly, because we are supposedly rested from our slumber and we should wake up relaxed and at peace. However, this is not the case for many of us. Many of us wake up and start thinking about everything we have to do in the day, even before we allow ourselves the space to gently get out of bed and start fresh, revived and ready to take on the world.

Some of us look at our email or social media shortly after opening our eyes, or we get confused and unfocused for other reasons. Therefore, meditation for twenty minutes early in the morning helps us clear our mind, relax our nervous system, and allow our brains to gently wake up and be ready for the day. I wanted to create a place for me when I traveled. I wanted to create a place that would allow me to keep my meditation practice wherever I was. This way I could stay calm, focused, reach my goals, and not be distracted.

When you travel, your schedule and itinerary look

completely different. One thing I figured would be consistent is that I would have to sleep, which meant that I could meditate in bed before I actually had to get up to start my day. I always suggest meditating in bed twenty minutes before you get up, which factors in only five minutes for actual meditation and the other fifteen minutes to gently wake yourself up. It works great, and it clears your mind for your morning routine, wherever you find yourself.

This is a great place for beginners to start their practice, and it is also great for anyone who meditates and struggles with keeping their practice up when they travel. When you get more advanced and you want to take your meditation to higher levels, you will likely want to look for a well-established routine and place to meditate on a regular basis.

SOMETIMES WE HAVE AMAZING, supportive people around us who just get it, but unfortunately that is not always the case. For example, because I grew up as one of the youngest in a big family, it was hard for my older siblings to understand what I needed, because they were so focused on their own needs. Therefore, I would not say that this was a very supportive environment, though it was no one's fault. Sometimes, it just is what it is. I would try to find ways to have that time for myself however I could. Studying for school was always a good way for me to get peace and quiet. And studying at four o'clock in the morning ensured that I had plenty of peace and quiet.

It is possible that some of our family, friends, or loved

ones do not like change. They could feel awkward if you are trying to meditate around them. If this is the case for you, no worries; simply try to pick a place that works for you and doesn't cause you to have to explain to others what you are embarking on. Of course, soon others will start to notice that you are different—not in any physical way, but rather different in that you may start to come across as more relaxed.

When you are more relaxed, you will deal with stressful situations differently. People may be pleasantly surprised and wonder what you are doing. Not to worry; as you meditate more, you will also learn to be more aware and caring of others, even of those who do not like change and may be confused by your emerging sense of self-confidence.

Meditation is life-changing, and when you look at it that way, finding your place for the practice becomes easy, because you want to experience those benefits right away. A result of beginning a meditation practice is that your relationships will become more loving and meaningful. When we take care of ourselves, we are also taking care of others. We cannot get better and feel better without acting better—it just does not work that way. When we feel better, we think better, and when we think better, we treat ourselves and others better.

Find peace. Peace is relaxing and it puts us in a state of flow. For me, time stops when I am doing something I absolutely love. You can meditate anywhere, and when you start your practice wherever you choose, you will soon

PICK YOUR PLACE

realize that you can meditate in more places than you ever thought possible, do more activities while meditating than you ever thought possible.

Since I picked up a meditation practice as a habit, it is showing up everywhere in my life. Not only that, I am feeling so much happier and more fulfilled. For example, when I talk to my children, I am more relaxed and I give them more space. When my husband and I talk, I allow him to have his voice, and I do not try to figure out what he is trying to say, but I ask questions and also give him the space to tell me what is on his mind. Space is something meditation gives me, and I in turn give space to my family members and others. These are the gifts that await you as well when you start your meditation practice.

When we take care of ourselves, we are also taking care of others.

Though every situation is different, I know that meditation is extremely beneficial, and for you to start doing it is vital to your happiness, peace of mind, and clarity. There are so many benefits to meditating, and I see them more clearly after decades of meditation. I am writing early in the morning with no distractions, I have some meditation music on, it is quiet and peaceful right now, and I feel amazing. When I meditate I clear my mind, and when I clear my mind, I can easily see what the next step in life should be.

When I first started meditating again, I did not put much thought into it. I truly think that meditation, because it can be so vast and complicated, can also be elusive, and this is why I decided to dedicate my life to creating meditation as a habit. It finally helped me relax on a regular basis, not just sometimes here and there, but all the time. I mostly meditated wherever I was when I felt that I needed to get some stress relief or if I wanted to feel relaxed before I had something important to do.

I found myself meditating in my office powder room; they had stalls for privacy, and they were clean and basically empty, so that worked for me after college. I also found myself meditating on walks from my office. I would do the breathing exercises while walking. Sometimes, I would do some meditating in my car; after I reached my destination, I would sit in my car for several minutes and do some breathing work.

From my experience, you can meditate anywhere at any time. The practice in this book of meditation through breathing is for the beginner. The act of breathing is extremely important, so much so that experts in many fields recommend it, such as Dr. Rangan Chatterjee, whom I quoted at the beginning of this chapter.

Deep breathing on its own can be extremely helpful, and for someone to do simple deep breathing can in fact help the nervous system relax. But when you are breathing under the umbrella of meditation, it takes on a whole new meaning, and more importantly, a whole new form for your overall health, wellness, and happiness. The way we are using breathing here is to relax your brain, mind, body, and soul.

PICK YOUR PLACE

THE WAY I AM TALKING about breathing in this book is different from the way some of the psychology communities or deep-breathing communities would have you do your breathing exercises.

For example, if you are doing deep breathing work, meaning you are taking deep breaths in and out, then this type of practice could be a bit loud. It is a completely amazing practice and I highly recommend it if you would like to eventually work up to it; however, this type of breathing practice is hard to do out in public. So what I am suggesting is simply doing gentle breathing exercises for five minutes, which provide all the benefits of deep breathing. I would know: it's this exact practice that helped me get rid of my migraines.

Try your best to shed your self-consciousness while doing these exercises. Most people are so busy doing their best with their own lives that they will not even notice that you have started meditation breathing exercises, or even that you have taken up meditation as part of your life. This is good news, as it will help you reap the benefits of doing a meditation practice anywhere and at any time of day. It is so subtle that you can also do it as many times in the day as you would like. Anywhere means anywhere! You can be as creative or as practical as you want. You are the one that is in the driver's seat of your meditation practice, so just enjoy this little gem of a meditation and let its gifts start working for you.

MEDITATION

LET'S TAKE OUT the word "MEDITATION" from wherever you stored it last.

Did you pull it out since last time we met, or did you have time to take it out and hold it in the palm of your hand again to look at it and inspect it some more, to see how you felt about it?

Now let's hold it in the palm of our hands again.

In Abraham Hicks's "Guided Meditation Deep Sleep" on YouTube, she talks about the cute little "MEDITATION" we are all holding in the palms of our hands.

She says the following:

> Meditation is the practice of "Quieting Your Conscious Mind."
> *(Your conscious mind can be likened to the virtual memory on your computer: all the windows you have open right now and are currently working on.)*
>
> Meditation allows you to tap into your "Unconscious Mind."
> *(Your unconscious mind would be like your hard drive or long-term memory. This is where every-*

PICK YOUR PLACE

thing you think and everything you do comes from; it is like the apps and systems you have on your hard drive in your computer that you call on and open in your virtual memory to use them.)

Meditation is transformational: "It Allows You To Tap Into What You Truly Want."

(When we meditate, we can quickly close or quiet our mind. This gives us instant relief. We can then open only what we need to work on and avoid being overwhelmed by having too many windows open.)

Meditation helps us get refocused on our needs: "It Allows Us To Be Mentally Clear."

(Some ingredients for becoming stressed are having a contradictory mind, often because we do not know what to do next due to too many thoughts.)

I know the example above may seem a little convoluted, but the most important takeaway about "MEDITATION" is the power it has to quickly diffuse stress and move you toward peace and tranquility. That little gem you are holding in the palm of your hand, "MEDITATION," has that much power.

QUESTIONS

- What do you think about the fact that you can

change your state of mind immediately through "MEDITATION?"
- What times do you think are the most beneficial for you to meditate?
- What do you think about the idea that "MEDITATION" has been around for thousands of years and the people who meditated thousands of years ago were getting the same results you could be getting today?

03
METHOD

"The science is clear. It works. People come up to me with questions like, 'Should I breathe through the nose?' or 'The diaphragm this or that,' and I just say, 'Yeah, breathe, motherfuckers! Don't think, just do it! Get into the depth of your own lungs!' Because all you have to do to reap the benefit of the method is to do it. You will feel transformed in minutes, after a few rounds of breathing. So get out of your mind and get into your breath, because the breath is the life-force. Not your mind, the breath. Follow your breath, and it will lead you anywhere in your brain—thus the mind—that you want to go."

—Wim Hof, *The Wim Hof Method*[9]

Coming from a large family where I was given no clear direction and joining corporate America after college was a big change for me. I worked for some small startups and insurance agencies, which were good companies, but I was easily bored, as I was not ready to simply relax and wine and dine people. Don't get me wrong; the opportunities and companies were amazing, but it was not the right fit for me at the time.

I ended up in investment banking and finance, which was a dynamic environment that I absolutely loved. It was a bit shocking for me, as I was an English and Rhetoric double major from UC Berkeley, so ending up in the finance sector was odd, at best. I agreed to take a position at an investment banking firm in the equity research department, even though I felt that I could not offer them a finance background or even any finance experience. The pay was very lucrative, as well as the environment. There were lots of young professionals from top financial schools, so I felt that I had hit the jackpot. I was a good hire, and I knew this. It was just a bit stressful, because many of the people here were solid finance professionals who had studied specifically for these jobs.

Long story short, it was hard and I felt the pressure—but also the exhilaration. Investment banking can be dynamic in that it has to deal with information constantly, and this is exciting. But it also means anything can happen at any time. Our job in the research department was to read the ribbons that brought the news. We had to review those daily, hourly, to find out if any of our companies were in the news. What really stood out for me was my need to find a way to balance the stress.

It was during this time that I wanted to look for a yoga studio so I could start doing my yoga meditation on a regular basis; I felt it would help me stay level-headed in such a dynamic environment. The yoga meditation classes would be an outlet for all the energy that was flowing around us. I tried some studios, but they did not focus on breathing so much as poses, so I did not get the benefit I was searching for at that time in my life. If at this time I had known that the real power was in the breathing, I could have just done this on my own at home and reaped the rewards earlier on.

Meditation can be done in so many ways. The one thing that I do know about meditation is that there must be a relaxation aspect to it. It does not matter if the meditation practice is the most advanced or the simplest form of meditation; you have to start by being relaxed, and this relaxation starts with your breath and breathing. We are all already breathing, every single one of us.

Wim Hof's experience with breath is a beautiful story; he uses breathing as a transformational tool to help people not only become healthier, but also feel younger and more resilient. The simple act of breathing in an intentional way can be transformational and can help you find self-actualization. It seems too simple to be true, but it is.

Before UC Berkeley, I did not think about my breath. The only times I thought about my breath were when I was holding it to try to disappear so I would not get in trouble. This makes perfect sense, because in between the fear of getting in trouble with my mother as a child, and holding my breath in order to touch the bottom of a deep pool, there was really no other time I thought about it.

I could count the times I thought about my breath in childhood on one hand. When I went to the UC Berkeley yoga meditation class, I was a complete beginner. Even

THE POWER OF BREATH

after taking that workshop and learning how it worked, breathing was still elusive to me because I connected breathing with the practice of yoga. This meant that for me to meditate meant I was under the impression that I had to learn and do yoga in order to get the breathing benefits I experienced that one time.

I enrolled in yoga classes, and I also bought books on meditation. That first instructor in yoga meditation was a great and powerful instructor, truly helping all the students achieve peace and tranquility. However, the yoga classes I signed up for later on did not all live up to that first experience. The books I bought on meditation were cumbersome and intense, and half the time I had no clue what they wanted me to do. They stressed me out more than they relaxed me. This was unfortunate because, although I loved the practice and I knew that it could help me, I was not getting any results. Alas, I gave up in annoyance.

No matter how much we have practiced, we are all beginners.

Like me, you could be a person that has tried to learn how to meditate, but the whole process of finding a class that fits with instructors who are great at their work is a big task. But do you just give up? No. Your health and your happiness are way too important for you to say, *Too bad, this meditation is not for me.*

For beginners or people who have dabbled in meditation but maybe left the practice as it became way too complicated, this is your sign to get back on the path of

METHOD

having a meditation practice. As I briefly mentioned earlier, the beginner's meditation practice we are looking at is extremely basic. No matter how much we have practiced, we are all beginners.

Sure, we can be experts at certain subjects, jobs, and the like. However, part of having a meditation practice is that you are open to learning more about yourself and about what you need. This mentality will help you as a person. It will help you be happier, healthier, and more successful. We can call ourselves experts, because if we have tapped into our inner world we are the true experts of ourselves. But we can also take this a step further and say: we are experts of ourselves with a beginner's mindset—a growth mindset. I call myself an expert of myself with a beginner's mindset as well.

The road of meditation is a lifelong journey. Just as when you were a child and you were curious, this curiosity is mindful and present, a real thing you can tap into at any age, time, or place. When you look at something with a beginner's mindset, you look at something in its present form, and in looking at things in this way, you can always gather something new and interesting. This also helps your mind relax; you breathe and let things be as they will be, nothing more and nothing less. Meditation practice will help you with the relaxation part. We keep learning because this way we keep moving forward.

As beginners, the method we want to use for our meditation practice is breathing. The reason we choose breathing as our method is that it is the most accessible to all of us. I would imagine at one point in your life you have thought about your breathing or actually have done some breathing exercises.

When I was younger, breathing was never a topic that got a lot of attention from me, unless I was doing something like trying to hide from my mom. I remember she loved to sew and would buy lots of fabric. As a young child, I enjoyed all manner of projects. I loved to watch my mom use her creativity. She would sew, garden, and do floral arrangements, and she enjoyed designing in general.

I also found I enjoyed doing most of this, mostly because it was all so artistic and pleasing to the eye. I loved to walk around our house and admire the floral arrangements or go outside on a sunny day and play in the garden. I especially enjoyed playing with my mother's fabric. I admired my mom, so I would try to do what she did with clothes and learn how to make it: cutting the fabrics into some kind of pattern, pretending I was going to make a blouse, a dress, shorts, whatever. I would get bored easily though, and leave all the pieces where they were. To this day I don't understand why I did stuff like that. I think I wanted to truly make something, but I did not have a real plan or anyone teaching me how to actually cut and sew. It would all be fine until she found all the scraps that I'd inevitably ruined under other, whole fabrics as she was working on a piece of her own.

I was never around when she actually found the fabric that I was using (thank goodness). However, I did know when she found the fabric I cut up because I would hear her yell from across the house, "Who cut my fabric?" That was usually my cue to run far away and hide. I would hide in her closet behind her clothes and try to hold my breath so she would not find me.

Of course, my mother knew very well that it was me and she would yell at me for a little while but then let me off the hook. I hid from her so she could get over her initial upset, because my mother was a firm believer in spanking. I was not okay with this, so I hid, slowed my breathing, and hoped she would get over it quickly. She would let me off with a warning that next time she wouldn't be so lenient. I laugh now, but it was very scary as a kid.

I also remember holding my breath when I was with my sister playing in the community pool in the summer. We had to hold our breath so we could race down and touch the bottom of the pool, twelve feet underwater. It was absolutely exhilarating when we held our breath until we got to the bottom of the pool, touched it, and jetted back up to the surface of the pool where we could breathe again. I loved playing this game with my sister; we would play for hours during the hot summers.

These are the only things I truly remember holding my breath for: hiding from my mother in the closet, and diving in the pool for hours and hours on scorching days.

HOW MANY OF US unknowingly walk around in a fight-or-flight state on a daily basis? What is a fight-or-flight state, anyway? When we had to find our own food out in the world and hunt and gather, we had to deal with many unknowns. Sometimes we had to literally fight with our environment, and often we ran into danger. Let's say a hungry animal invaded our environment. We wouldn't just stand there defenseless; we would do whatever we could to save our lives.

For example, a gazelle in the wilderness that is confronted by something that wants to eat it does not stand in place and relax *(rest and digest)*, but rather it runs away as fast as it can *(fight or flight)*. Humans also have this instinct to fall back on when we are in danger.

When researching the nervous system, I came across an article describing it as "a network of nerve cells and fibers which transmits nerve impulses between parts of the body."[10] In layman's terms, the nervous system is what sends the messages to the entire body and the brain. It basically acts like the local control, or the air control tower at an airport; your nervous system is overlooking your environment and body to keep you informed on what is needed.

The person managing the control tower at the airport is like your nervous system managing the information in your body. Whereas the person that is managing the airplane tower cannot always control what is happening in the sky, we can control our body's environment. For you and me, if we are dealing with habits of stress, trauma, or anything else that we unfortunately think is a real threat, or if whatever that is looping back and forth is causing us great stress and anxiety and keeping us in this sympathetic nervous system state, what do we do? This information is stuck in our body.

Let's hold that thought for a minute. Let's go back to where we were. Remember, our nervous system is basically going to give information in only two ways. The first part is the side that says, "Oh no, we have a problem, there is danger up ahead." This would be called the *sympathetic* nervous system. A problem or danger will alert the entire body so it can get ready for survival. This sympathetic nervous system alerts by creating stress so we act in whatever manner would help us survive. Stress would be paramount and important here in order for us to have a chance of survival.

The second way to receive information then would be the *parasympathetic* nervous system. This system is active when that gazelle is eating and relaxing in the warm sun. There is no danger, and the gazelle can rest and cool down. In our control tower analogy, it would be the equivalent of receiving a message like, "Everything looks good out here in the sky, everything is clear for landing and take off. The sun is shining and all planes are arriving and leaving out of the airport without a hitch." As we can see here, the parasympathetic nervous system is relaxed.

In my understanding of post-traumatic stress syndrome, it boils down to focusing on a traumatic part of one's life. One of my therapists in 2002 explained that what ends up happening is that trauma stays stuck in the body until it is allowed to move up and out.

She also explained that it is like a deer almost getting hit by a car: it freezes, and when the car stops, the deer unfreezes, SHAKES IT OFF, and then goes about its business. SHAKING IT OFF is the part that most people do not do, unless they go to therapy or have someone else help them understand what happened so they can move on. They must SHAKE OFF the trauma that has stayed in their bodies.

Psychologists do this in schools, especially in elementary schools when something tragic has happened in the community and the children hear about it. The community and the school psychologist ensure they help the children understand what happened and go through the emotions, feelings, and any questions that they have about the event so they can basically SHAKE IT OFF and stabilize their emotions. The idea is that if professionals can quickly walk the children through the event and deal with it openly in a supportive manner, then there is no confusion and the children will have a way of dealing with the stress, diffusing it, and then moving on, just as the deer did. It is when the stress is stuck in the body that it tends to manifest in our lives negatively; breathing helps release the stress.

I am oversimplifying things here again, and it is only for your benefit. Obviously, all situations and people are different, and maybe you need a little bit of help, or maybe you need a lot. Learning to meditate and breathing intentionally (just breathing and thinking about your breath is enough to be intentional) will most definitely help you get there.

We have established that you will have times when you need to be on high alert and all your systems are completely activated; you are anxious, on edge, you have tons of adrenaline and testosterone running through your body, you are basically ready for anything. You are "on," and this could be extremely stressful to your body if you are in this state for no reason all day long. Remember, we said that if there is a real threat, then to be in a sympathetic response is healthy and appropriate. At such times, being on high alert is not only wise, but life-saving.

But what happens when your parasympathetic nervous system is running your nervous system? Then it is a time to relax, to chill out.

When we think of both parts of the nervous system we can go a little deeper. The *sympathetic nervous system initiates the fight-or-flight* response and the *parasympathetic nervous system initiates the rest-and-digest* response. The sympathetic and parasympathetic nervous systems are important for your entire body's functions, breathing, and your overall circulatory and digestive systems.

Now let's go back to those old habits or traumas that may be stuck in the body. If they give false positives for danger being around when there is none, what do we do? Our bodies are receiving faulty, outdated information. The body doesn't know the difference between a real threat or a perceived threat caused by over-exhaustion or some other stimulus, so the body automatically triggers our fight-or-flight state. And when our bodies put us in this state on a regular basis, we feel irritable, upset, and simply drained. Whether the threat comes from an actual predator, as opposed to a looming deadline or too many planned activities, your brain doesn't want to take the chance.

Another key factor is that, because you are operating from the fight-or-flight mode, you are using tons and tons of energy—for what? If we think about it, when you are constantly running—metaphorically speaking—you are going to be tired. Even though nothing in the environment is actually going to attack you, nobody is sending out the memo to your system, alerting it that there is actually no real danger, that it is a false message, a glitch. But memo or no, once you are in fight-or-flight mode, it is serious business for your body. In fight-or-flight mode, there is no time to focus on your breathing.

> *Meditation is the memo to the body saying,* Hey, we are taking a break; we are okay.

In other words, meditation is the memo to the body saying, *Hey, we are taking a break; we are okay.*

When we are in fight-or-flight mode all the time, our immune system, relationships, and worldview are compromised. This fight-or-flight mode is now creating challenges for the same systems it is meant to protect.

Fight or flight means that our body's "air traffic controller" is unable to function. If it's on all the time, how are we going to get planes in and out of the airport? If the person manning the tower has constant disturbance, they can't do their job, and the airport won't be able to function correctly. Everything will have to stop, because planes can't take off and land when no one is overseeing the airspace. If there is a real problem, such as bad weather, thunder, or icy conditions on the runways, it makes sense for the airport to put the less urgent stuff on hold to deal with the pressing issues. But when the only problem is that the controller is in fight-or-flight mode for no real reason, the sky above the body's "airport" is going to get really crowded—dangerously so.

In my life, I have often been looking for a clear blue sky. One thing that happens when you are being raised in a home with so many children is that there are always thunderstorms or icy tarmacs. For one thing, the house is crowded. You are growing up with so many other children who are going through a plethora of different developmental states, and they are all trying to establish who they are. I absolutely loved having such a big family, but it was also exhausting. When something went awry, it was a complete one-eighty flip, and this could be traumatizing for a small child. Parents and older siblings were trying to do their best and trying to understand themselves and their needs, but my needs, since I was so young, seemed like an afterthought for everyone else.

I know this can sound like I did not get any attention, but I did get attention: sometimes a smack on my arm or head, and sometimes a warm, loving smile and a big hug. I never knew what I was going to get, and I was constantly nervous about it. With so many children in the house,

I also learned how to keep myself safe and survive my childhood.

Your story may be different, but one thing I know is that we all had some challenges growing up, whether from a big family, no family, something in between, or an instance later on in life that made you start "holding your breath" emotionally.

Now let's go back to the sympathetic or parasympathetic nervous system state. If we think of the sympathetic nervous system as the fight-or-flight state in which we mostly take shallow breaths, we could say that I was in this shallow breathing state for most of my childhood. I remember loving school, because I could finally find some relief from the chaos at home. I loved to play, so I usually had a good group of friends that I got to play with on a regular basis. I felt completely capable and confident with anything we were doing in school. School gave me the space to breathe; my parasympathetic nervous system was in the much-needed rest-and-digest phase.

I enjoyed school so much that they asked me if I wanted to be the street crossing patrol officer. The patrol officer had to get out of school earlier than the other students (this was not only an official title, but it was a very serious and important position for me). In my new positon, I would leave class a bit early and get my orange vest and stop sign at the office before proceeding to the crosswalk right outside of school. The patrol officer had to ensure that all students could cross the street safely.

When they had initially asked me to do it, I was in second grade, and I was so happy. Finally, someone saw how talented and useful I could be, because no one at home even knew I existed, it seemed to me.

It can be sad to think about. I would completely slip their minds; it was so bad that they would literally forget about me and leave me by myself at home. But not here at school—no, at school they knew I existed and they even asked me to hold the very prestigious and important role of crosswalk officer. These are special memories for a second-grader.

So what does this have to do with breathing and meditation? When I was at home, I was stressed out all the time, and I breathed very shallowly almost constantly. I liked to sleep and do homework, because at least then I could give myself some space away from the fray. However, sometimes I couldn't. Maybe one of my siblings was having a hard time with my mom or another sibling, and things would just escalate out of control. I felt so scared, sad, and angry when these things happened. I would try to stay out of it and try to keep myself safe, but sometimes it wasn't possible, because I had to help pick up the pieces of whatever was broken, emotionally or otherwise. It was miserable.

I hated this so much that my emotions would escalate and I would hide in the closet, literally wishing that I would be adopted and saved from the chaotic, hostile environment that was my home. Watching my siblings and my mom fight made me feel helpless and confused; I loved all of them and couldn't stand watching them be mean and hurtful to each other. I was stressed out all the time. I was the tiniest family member, and I felt hopeless.

Everyone in my home appeared to me as giants who were always doing this or that because there were no clear rules; things were handled in different ways every time, depending on who was involved and what options were on the table. This sounds so unclear and confusing, and that is exactly how I felt when I had to witness all of this—a lot of chaos and unclear energy, and so much unresolved tension on a daily basis. Think of *Lord of the Flies* (our home could turn this way in a second and then quickly change back, until the next thunderstorm hit). A lawless land in itself is traumatizing.

My siblings all had their own needs and wants. Everyone required something different for different reasons, and they all decided how they got what they needed. My mom was mostly a referee in our home; many times things seemed like they were okay until they were not, and then it would feel like an explosion. Though not an actual explosion, its impact on a child is pretty much the same thing: there were many casualties. It was hard to bear, and it was even harder because I was already home, supposedly a safe space, and where could I retreat to? Where could I go to take a much needed break? Spa day, anyone? Not!

Growing up thinking this was normal and how the world works was not much help. I definitely felt as if I needed more space, my own space. It was exceedingly exhausting, living in this type of environment. Don't get me wrong; there were a lot of fun times growing up, but I also remember being much too weary for my age. Chaos was and still is exhausting for me.

THE INSTANT YOU ARE in a fight-or-flight state, your whole system completely changes. Your breathing pattern slows down to a point where your whole world has basically stopped. This is the moment that makes every second feel like a minute, or even an hour long.

Everything you do feels like it's happening through a superhero lens. All people have this capability. The downside of this is that your body is using tons and tons of resources. If you are in this state for too long, your body will start to malfunction, and it can basically turn itself off in order to survive. Obviously, everything I am telling you here is extreme, so extreme that most people will never experience it, but I want to give you the full idea of how powerful your body can be and how important breathing is for your system.

Trying to find some distance between myself and my fight-or-flight mode was not an easy task. As I mentioned before, I would go into my mom's closet when I was younger. When I turned nine or ten, I started going into the closet that was in the bedroom that I shared with my sister. My mother's closet was large and ours was not, but I still loved to get in there and close the door and cry.

My mom's closet was a large closet for a little kid, and I liked to think that it was my own bedroom. Before I was nine, things were not as hard for me and I could go into

THE POWER OF BREATH

my mom's closet and relax a little. It was big enough for me to move around with ease, yet small enough to make me feel contained. It was the closest thing I found to my own sanctuary growing up.

At one point we moved from our very big house to a smaller house in a new neighborhood. During that transition, which took about two years, my mom had me live with my grandparents. I was without my siblings, alone. I loved this, because I not only got lots of love, but received much-needed attention as well. It was a little lonely not having all of my siblings, but I did like the peace and quiet.

I remember sitting down at my grandmother's kitchen table and helping her prepare food. She had me sit down and gave me a large bowl of pinto beans, saying, "Now what I need you to do is take out any rocks or other pebbles that may be in the beans, because we do not want these to be in there when we cook them." I nodded and was happy to help her, but I was also a kid and I did play with my food a little. I would place all the beans in rows to create a ranch with a fence, then within the fence I would have horses, cows, chickens, and ranchers. My grandmother would be working in the kitchen alongside me, and I had a great time.

I would also help my grandfather. He liked to plant tomatoes, chili peppers, and mint, and I loved to help him in the garden. I especially enjoyed looking through the tomatoes and finding the big, fat, green worms that were on the tomato vines. I do not know if these worms were good for the tomatoes or not. I never asked my grandfather, and he may have gotten rid of them on a regular basis, but I was fascinated by them. I remember thinking they were so beautiful.

Watching the tomatoes and chilis grow was amazing. They all had such wonderful colors and they were sweet-tasting and plump. I would even sample the wine grapes he planted in the back yard, which were extremely sour. I had fun eating those, anyway.

My grandparents allowed me to experience the rest-and-digest state, so I remembered that when I went back to my family's new home. Even though I was not doing breath work, I was still doing my best to quiet my mind in that closet. It wasn't a conscious choice, but the body sometimes knows you better than your brain does.

When I was around the age of nine, things started getting more real for me. It could also be because I was getting bigger and my siblings could no longer ignore me. During the next few years, my grandmother passed away and my grandfather stayed with us. Before this, some of my siblings started making many decisions as adults, and I think this is when things in our home started becoming unbearable for me; not because they were becoming adults, but rather the implications this had for my mom and our overall family dynamic. It was such a confusing environment, because everyone was trying to take power in the home without having to give it, and the energy was very tense.

I literally could not take the exhaustion of my household anymore. I was in the fifth grade when my grandfather came to live with us. Of course this came with problems, too: my grandfather was so loving, but some of my siblings were not respectful toward him. I absolutely loved my grandfather, so when my siblings would disrespect him, I felt crushed. More helpless feelings.

Luckily, my sister and I did a lot of activities outside the home. Thanks to her, I was able to get some relief from the pressures. By the time I was twelve and started playing proper sports in school, I stopped hiding in the closet.

Although I did not recognize it at the time, I was actively searching for that rest-and-digest state somewhere, which happened to be the closet. I was looking for some relief from the fight-or-flight nervous system. I guess I could call that meditation. Even though I took the quiet time—and this was mostly before I learned to play volleyball and basketball and run track—I needed a way to release some of the stress and exhausting energy from being in fight-or-flight mode all the time.

WE ALL HAVE TO BREATHE. When we are no longer breathing, we are no longer alive. I want to share with you a sad story about my little Yorkshire terrier, who was named Einstein. I loved my little Einstein; he was not only a little adorable dog, but he also enjoyed giving love. He had a very silly personality and loved to get my attention by being playful. He would get in front of me and stare at me, and this usually meant that he wanted to play. He would literally stare at me until I played with him—it didn't take much for me to give in. I loved this about him,

METHOD

because he always made me laugh, and who doesn't want a good laugh?

Einstein also loved to go on walks. I would take him often, and he loved to get into the rhythm. He would get a little pep in his step and often looked like a little puppy, moving side to side like a little wind-up dog. It was beyond adorable when he did this, and it always made me smile.

The walks with Einstein were meditation, in a sense. We would be moving along, enjoying the trees, the cool crisp air, and the relaxing pace.

Einstein and I played a game where I would get down on the floor and tease him. I would gently grab his little front legs. He would start jumping from side to side as if there was some real serious stuff going on and start to bark in excitement. He would go back and forth and get into my space so I could grab for his front legs again. I would laugh, because it was such a riot. He was so animated, and he would let out little barks and then repeat; he would do the jumping from side to side and then come back for more. We both absolutely loved that game. He was a very gentle little dog, so loved and adored.

Why "Einstein"? When we went to look at the litter of dogs, we saw him, and his hair was a big mess, all up in the air and crazy looking, like the famous pictures of Albert Einstein. So when we picked our puppy, we called him Einstein for his crazy hairdo. I think he lived up to his name.

Unfortunately, we had to put our little Einstein to sleep. It was something I was fortunate enough to be there for. He was sixteen years old, and he had been having very serious health issues for the past three years, in addition to simply getting old. Six weeks prior, Einstein had started to slow down; he mostly wanted to sleep, and when I would take him on our walks, he always wanted to immediately turn around and come back home. I actually started carrying him for some of the walks, just so he could get out for a bit.

The day came when he got very sick and we took him in to the animal hospital; the veterinarian told us Einstein did not have long to live. I think I already intuitively knew that he was not doing well and that our days with Einstein were numbered, but I did not realize how close to the end he was. Our little Einstein would be leaving us and would soon have his last rite of passage. I was in disbelief from the grief of having to lose my little furry friend, my little companion for the past sixteen years.

When we took him in and the veterinarian said he was in critical condition, I did not know how to handle the information, because it did not seem real. I was in disbelief. My mind sort of shut down because I could not handle the pain of the news. It was so bad that my initial instinct was to tell my husband to have the vet put him to sleep then and there. My children were not happy with this decision, since they wanted to see him for one last time before we said goodbye. The pain was unbearable, but I knew Einstein was suffering, more and more.

I felt horrible for Einstein, for myself, and for my family. My husband wanted to bring Einstein home one last time, and I did some research on the internet to try to

METHOD

figure out if I could get ahold of my feelings and come up with a solution that made sense to all of us under the dire circumstances.

I just typed into Google, "Should the pet owner be there when the dog is put to sleep due to illness?" There were all sorts of sites, so I read about five different random articles, and what I found is that most agreed it would be good to be there with your animal, because they know you are there for them. I decided that I wanted to be there for our little Einstein. We ended up bringing him home for one last night.

I was torn. I had never had to deal with this before. I did not know what to do, and my family had mixed feelings about it as well. The best thing to do in this situation is to be there for your pet when they are going to be put to sleep. I found an article that claimed it's important to have the family there for the pet's last rite of passage.[11] It is better for the pet to know that the family is there for them in their passing and for the family to be there with them so they are comforted. When I read this I immediately told my family we would be there for Einstein in his final moments, no matter what.

Since we decided to be there for Einstein, we were happy we had brought him home for his final night. I made him his favorite food. We wrapped him in a warm blanket like a baby, and we carried him everywhere, always looking into his eyes and telling him we were sorry he was so sick. We also told him how much we loved him and how much he meant to all of us. He would just stare back into our eyes as if saying *I love you,* and we would cry, but we were mostly happy that we could hold him and comfort him on his last day. He was always full of so much love; he found great joy in being part of our family, and we had sixteen years of fun memories with him. It felt good to just be able to hold and soothe him.

The next day, the family said their final goodbyes to Einstein. My husband and I were the only ones allowed in the room with Einstein, as we were under COVID restrictions. Our kids were way too sad anyway, so I guess it was a small blessing.

When the kids were saying their goodbyes they were crying, and I know Einstein did not like to see the kids sad, so he would move around and try to get out of his blanket as if to say, *Hey kids, don't worry, I am okay;* which was not the truth, but he still was trying to make everyone happy.

It was such a dramatic turnaround that I actually second-guessed our decision. I was thinking of getting the vetenarian to call off the whole thing. We ended up calling our good friend, who works with dogs that are critically sick, and when we asked her if she thought that Einstein might actually be all right, she said, "No, he just wants you to remember him as the fun-loving dog you know him to be." This was devastating, but we eventually had to face the situation head-on.

I was holding Einstein as if he were a newborn baby, all wrapped in a blanket, and he was feeling nice and cozy. He would look at us with his caring eyes, and despite our sadness we felt good that we would be with him for his last breath, keeping him warm and comfortable in our arms. While we sat with Einstein, we stroked the hair between his eyes gently. We sat with him for a little while and we were instructed to push a button when we were ready for the veterinarian to come into the room to perform the actual procedure.

We were at peace that we were there with him. We were grateful, and we gave him the love and support we always enjoyed from his company, all the love he showed us and all the love he gave us on a daily basis.

We finally rang the bell for the veterinarian to come in and perform the procedure. The vetenarian came in and asked us if we were ready. Einstein looked like he was at peace.

Then, it was done; she checked his vitals and he was gone. He took his final breath with us holding him in our lap, calm and looking very relaxed. They told us to stay as long as we liked. We stood for a few minutes, but then we were overwhelmed with sadness and we were ready to leave.

Einstein took his last breath. He left us. I was in a lot of pain and disbelief that I would not see my little Einstein again, my little companion for the last sixteen years. Now he was gone. Rest in peace, Einstein. We love you. I felt inspired to put a very simple poem together for my little buddy. This poem is dedicated to Einstein, from me:

"Breathe
Breathing

THE POWER OF BREATH

Breath
Einstein, We Loved You So
We Are So Sad to Let You Go
Breathe
Breathing
Breath
Einstein, Your Breath, Your Breath."

Breathing, breath, inhalations, in and out. This is what some people do not really think about. To be fair, I never truly thought about my breath until I learned about it at Berkeley. But there, in that veterinarian's office, I learned about breathing. I had never been with any of my pets for their last breath until Einstein. I think just being there with my little buddy, knowing that he was suffering, I knew that to help him we had to allow him to go.

It was so raw, to think that I was never going to see him again, that he no longer would be breathing. It helped me put my own breathing into focus. I had learned that my little Einstein was gravely sick, and I learned that I could make the decision to help Einstein by taking away his breath so he would not suffer anymore. This powerful thing called breath is something we take for granted because we don't have to think about it. It is just there and it just happens. Breathing.

We were able to bring him home, we could properly say our goodbyes to little Einstein, and we were there to help him go through the journey from this life to the next. We were there for his last breath. He performed his last

METHOD

rite of passage in that last exhalation.

Breathing is the easiest form of meditation. And it is not only the easiest, but the most vital, and everyone knows how to do it. We all breathe, and breath is very powerful.

Moreover, when we think of breathing as the most natural part of being alive, then it makes sense that we all already have access to this gift. And because breath is instinctive, the simplest form of meditation, then don't we all already know how to meditate on some intrinsic level?

Einstein's story shows that if we are not breathing, we are no longer in this world. Hence, you are breathing if you are reading this book, so you're basically halfway there. And breathing is meditation. Now, if we simply learn some new ways of inhaling and exhaling, or if we stop to think about our breathing for just five minutes every day, then we are truly doing a meditation practice. Voila! You are a guru; a meditation master. Meditating is easy-peasy.

Remember: what you do with your breath is magical. You can give your body, soul, and mind much-needed relaxation and peace. You can get all that simply from meditation, simply from breathing, and you can check that off your meditation to-do list.

BREATHING IS SO AUTOMATIC, most of us do not even give it a second thought. This is why we take our breath for granted. For example, for the longest time I did not realize I had breath. I did not acknowledge that breathing was even a thing. I never even thought about it.

Why would I think about breath and breathing? That question sounds ludicrous. It is only when something is going on with us that we start to think about our breath, but most of us walk around this Earth clueless as to what is going on with it.

In my early years, I never had any interest in breathing patterns or thinking about my breath, let alone paying attention to my breath for any amount of time. No one ever talked to me about my breath until UC Berkeley, but even this was coupled with other exercises. These are two very big topics, so even here, breath and breathing is blanketed and covered by these two other intricate words: yoga and meditation. Even as I learned about yoga and meditation, I did not truly learn about breathing. I think because we do it all the time, we think, *Don't fix what ain't broke*. We think, *I breathe just fine, so what is there to do anyway?*

Breathing is part of being alive, and it just happens unconsciously. But let's think about it now. Breathing is literally the first thing we do when we start our lives. It even happens before we can take our first big cry to say, HELLO, WORLD. It goes like this: baby enters the world, breathes, and then cries—or, like my second child did, lets everyone in the room know that the journey here was okay, but not stellar. Breath first, everything else after.

We know that the brain is taking care of most of the breathing work in the background without our having to think about anything; your brain is constantly trying to take care of you. Since our breath is so important, don't you think we owe it to ourselves to find out a little more about our breathing and give it more attention? Breathing is so important that taking some inventory about how ours is working is a great idea. For example, once we start to notice our breathing and start to learn about it, it will give us a lot of information about ourselves and what we need in this world. One way that I am suggesting is that we start to learn about our breath by taking five minutes a day to simply focus on our breathing. I think that simply learning about your breath for five minutes a day is an amazing start to a lifelong journey.

Breath first, everything else after.

Spending five minutes a day focused on our breath will give us a lot of information about how we are currently breathing. The other benefit we will get is that we will start learning to relax whenever and wherever we find ourselves. Since your brain is always working, when you do five minutes a day of breathing exercises, this gives your brain a small break. It's essentially five minutes of down time. Your brain will reap the rewards of getting an actual break, and you will soon begin to feel the benefits because they are fairly immediate.

During these five minutes, your brain will be able to get rid of non-important items on your to-do list and come back with focused attention on what is truly needed. This is beneficial for two reasons: one, you will have more clarity; and two, you will not waste your time and energy working on something that is not important to you. It is especially easy for you to do the things you need to do when you do not have a lot of needless distractions and useless items on your to-do list. Meditation helps you clear the clutter!

MEDITATION

What I want you to do is just quiet your mind.

I want you to gently take a look at your breathing.

Just look at it: How is it happening in your body?

Are you having an easy time with it? Can you find it?

Is your breathing strong or is it soft?

What do you think of when you think about breath and breathing?

Do you feel comfortable talking about your breath?

Have you ever thought about your breath? Why or why not?

Okay, now just repeat the following to yourself:

Breathing, breath, breathe, breathing, breath, breathe, relax, relax.

METHOD

Breathing, breath, breathe, breathing, breath, breathe, relax, relax.

How did that feel? There is no right answer; it is simply your own personal experience with the words "Breath" and "Relax."

QUESTIONS

- Do you find it hard to start new things because you feel they will be difficult? Do you have a beginner's mindset?
- How often are you in fight-or-flight mode?
- How often do you think about your breath in a day?

04

HORMONES

> *"It will have its time in the rightful order of things."*
> —Alexandra Pope and Sjanie Hugo Wurlitzer,
> *Wild Power*[12]

Boy, did I go through some serious hormonal imbalances during my teenage years! I was always so confused and a bit scared at how much energy I would get—surges of it. I sometimes felt like the Incredible Hulk. And no, this was not in the powerful, cool way; I would ask myself, *What the hell is happening to me? Why do I have all this power? It is not healthy or safe for me to have all this power.*

I made it my job to figure out how to not only hone this energy, but to also use it wisely and with respect for myself and others. Hormones are extremely important and vital to all of us, and if they are out of sync because we do not understand them or do not take good care of ourselves, then they could harm us in different ways.

I recently read *Wild Power* by Pope and Wurlitzer, and it was at a time when I was doing a month of meditation to help me focus on my book and my commitment to meditating; it helped me understand myself and my hormones so much better. I learned that I could be okay with not being okay. The book actually explained a lot of questions I had about myself and my hormones, how truly powerful and necessary they were for my survival while I was growing up.

It is interesting that as I learn more about myself and how I work, I find that I can appreciate the process of being human so much more and I can be more vulnerable and lovable because I let myself be authentic while letting others do so as well. As I learn to love myself much more, I also learn to love others much more. This love is a clear love, an appreciation for myself and my journey, as well as an appreciation for others and their journeys. I love that I can now truly hold a beautiful and gracious space for others in a wholeheartedly gentle way. We are all just trying to do our best, every single one of us, but truth was tough for me as a child because I always thought I had to be perfect, and so did everyone else. Judgement of self and others on a second-by-second basis is unhealthy, and I knew there had to be a better way to live.

I always felt that I had to be alert, because I had to ensure that I was doing things the right way; making mistakes was never an option. I started doing this as a child and this is likely why I was exhausted all the time. As a preteen and an adult, I kept trying to out-do myself, and this was exhausting. Now I just pace myself, do what I need to get done, and try to enjoy the ride. I finally learned to genuinely enjoy myself from all my self-development and self-awareness work.

Breathing was a huge part of my work. The quality of your breathing is what helps you meditate, and this in turn improves your health. It helps you lower your cortisol and helps you rest and digest. What does that mean?

As we have previously discussed, when we breathe in a shorter breath than we breathe out, we are letting our body know that we are in rest-and-digest mode. This is a deeper breath than the usual shallow breaths we take throughout the day.

Say you breathe in for three seconds, hold your breath for four seconds, and breathe out for five seconds, hold your breath for two seconds, then repeat. When you do this, you will notice that when you breathe out, you must do it for longer, so this means that your breath out will take more concentration from you.

There are people walking around out there who do this out of habit, making this their default way to breathe. They force themselves to be mindfully present instead of living in the future or the past. Additionally, if they do this type of breathing, then they are constantly going to be in rest-and-digest mode, meaning they are going to be at peace with themselves and the world.

Usually, the people that are doing deeper breathing as opposed to shallow breathing are very easy to recognize. They usually appear very serene. They give off a feeling of peace when we are around them. They can be linked to a nice warm summer day or a gentle creek of fresh water running through a forest. It is as if you are watching a soft breeze gently move the leaves on a tree; it makes you feel so calm, as if all is well in the world. The energy they emit is gentle, relaxing, and peaceful. I absolutely love that state, and I wish that every single person could feel that loving peace within themselves.

Longer breaths out and shorter breaths in is the land of rest-and-digest, whereas shorter breaths in and out are what you get when you are in fight-or-flight mode. How can your breathing determine if you are in either fight-or-flight mode or rest-and-digest mode? This is a great question, and it has taken me a long time to figure this out for myself.

In my journey of self-discovery, self-awareness, and unconditional self-love, I have learned that breathing is very intricate, and the body and the mind are not always in sync. This means that if your body and your mind are not having open communication, you are not being honest with yourself and there is so much stuff you need to learn and discover about yourself. Meditation is a door to getting to know yourself, whether it be for the first time or to get reacquainted.

A lot of this has to do with hormones, specifically cortisol. We have many hormones that we create through the food we eat, our stress levels, and our environments. The scientific topic of cortisol is beyond the scope of this book, therefore, I will mainly talk about cortisol and how it can be a detriment to your health. If your body is typically at elevated levels, it means you are basically living in a state of fight-or-flight without even being aware of it.

If you are interested in learning more about the topic of hormones your body produces and would like an introductory-level, easy read on the subject, you can read Dr. Rangan Chatterjee's book, *How to Make Disease Disappear*, as he goes into more detail on hormones and explains how they affect your health. I will be talking about cortisol at a superficial level, mostly as it relates to learning about the benefits of meditation and how it could help improve your life, for the sake of your health and happiness.

WHEN MY HUSBAND AND I had initially moved to the Great Northwest, we were a young married couple. We had a child that was not one year old yet, and we found ourselves in a new state, a new house, new jobs, and a new community. There was a lot of newness going on around us.

I am the type of person who likes to find solutions to any challenge that comes my way. Well, all this newness was a bit too much for me. I felt a bit awkward being a new mom in a new house and being in an environment where I did not know much about anything. I had to find new grocery stores, new classes for my child, to meet new people at my new job, and figure out a new plan for my life. I both loved and feared it.

I knew that I was struggling with the move more than my husband was. He had many friends that he had worked with, and I had lost all of my other mom friends along with the activities my child was in, and even my business that I had been building for the past two years before our move. Don't get me wrong, I was happy with the move; the house and the neighborhood were wonderful, the area was absolutely beautiful, and there were a ton of career opportunities available. It was amazing and exciting, but I still had to deal with getting all of my outside resources in order, and this was a bit challenging for me. My husband wanted to be helpful, and he was enthusiastic about the move and the opportunity it held for our entire family.

I think one of the hardest things for me was having to deal with being a nursing mother. I wanted my child to be healthy and happy, and since I was nursing and already strung tight, it was hard for me to just relax. I would think, *I need to relax, I am trying to relax, I am not relaxing . . . Shit, I am not relaxing! What do I do?* That is not a relaxing cycle to be in; if anything, the act itself is bringing the body much more stress. Just acknowledging that I was doing my best would have helped me get those rest-and-digest hormones a mother wants when she is nursing her baby.

All of these things were adding more stress to my already stressful life. I know my husband wanted to be there for me, and I knew that I truly wanted to relax, but as my luck would have it, I also wanted to have everything figured out yesterday, which would only stress me out more. I was a perfectionist, so everything had to be flawless. A constant stream of, *I want to do "everything right" for my child* played like a record in my head. Now, if this record player in my brain was not causing my hormones to get out of wack, I do not know what was. This messaging was causing me a lot of stress.

I intuitively knew that my husband was trying hard to help me. He was doing his best and being as loving and caring as he could. Despite this, I remember thinking that agreeing to move here was a bad idea. I knew that I did it because it would be good for our entire family, but that fact was not helping me at the time. We were stressed out. We were both in new situations, and neither of us knew how to communicate or comfort each other. We knew we wanted to, but we each had so many new things coming at us that we were merely trying to get our bearings in our new environment.

During this time, I felt that my husband and I were having some challenges we couldn't surmount ourselves, and I wanted to seek professional help. My husband was not into therapy, so I thought going to a seminar with lots of other couples would work better for us, since we would be around many other couples seeking to improve their relationships, just as my husband and I were. Both my husband and I have a growth mindset, so we do not mind asking for help when we have a challenge. This is a good quality in our marriage.

Before we moved I used to see a therapist. She was able to help me when I initially moved out; however, at that time, having phone sessions for therapy was not something she offered. She encouraged me to find someone local to see, so we spoke for a final month and then I was no longer able to use her help.

THE POWER OF BREATH

The idea of finding a new therapist sounded fine, but I was also trying to find classes for my toddler and get familiar with my new grocery stores, classes for me, and a ton of other things. Most of them were for my baby. I was trying to find a pediatrician and get my doctor's appointments set up for all the checkups that are required for the first year. Not to mention I had to shop for diapers, toys, books, and anything else that I would need for my child. I also had to find other mothers to set up playdates with.

All this pressure I was putting on myself was stressing me out. I was so stressed that once I dropped a bottle of olive oil and it spilled all over the kitchen floor, and I was so frazzled that I literally thought it was the end of the world. I immediately called my husband and told him, "I don't know what to do, I just dropped all the olive oil all over the kitchen floor." Really? Wow. I laugh at this now, but I will tell you it was no laughing matter for a frazzled mom who forgot how to meditate, a frazzled mother who didn't know how to get back to rest-and-digest.

I know much of this had to do with my cortisol. If I had done some breathing that I had learned at UC Berkeley, maybe I could have handled this with grace and seen that it was not a big deal at all. It pretty much all boiled down to not being able to let go. It had to do with not being able to just relax and not understanding that what I was going through was normal and that my reactions were okay. If I had done some breathing work, I would have felt worlds better. But I did not breathe and meditate, so I was still in fight-or-flight mode.

My need to seek outside help was because I was afraid I would begin resenting my husband and blame him for the move. As I said, I knew that he was trying very hard to be there for me and help me. I knew that much of this stress was coming from me, from old habits, and from having ideas in my mind that were not helpful to a healthy relationship. I often did not know how to handle my overwhelmed feelings, so I lashed out at my husband.

I do want to mention that I had gone to therapy before I had children because I did not want to replay my upbringing. I wanted to be a mother who would manage my emotions and my temper. I did not want to hit my children and later feel horrible because of it. I was breaking the cycle.

Although my mother did a fabulous job in many respects, she also did some seriously hurtful things. When she was overwhelmed she would lash out at us, oftentimes physically. Her levels of cortisol and stress would reach insane proportions until she could not handle herself. Unfortunately, I was the recipient of this twice, but I always stood away from her, especially if things were chaotic in the house. I also saw other family members receive her pain, and this always hurt me emotionally.

I felt sad for myself and my siblings, who had to endure this treatment, and I also felt sad for my mother, who was the one losing her mind while she lashed out at us. I know some of you think that there is no excuse for hurting those you love in that way, and I agree with you. This was not okay, and there is no good reason for it, so that is why I decided I would never do it myself. My vow was to not hurt others, even if I was so angry that I could not see straight. I know that I was hurt, and it is so easy to fall into that cycle again, but I hated to see people in pain, so I vowed to avoid it at all costs.

So, fast-forward to being in this new environment, starting to lash out at my husband, almost becoming the person I swore I would not be. I was upset with the move because I felt that I did not have people I could decompress with, while my husband had a whole support system in place. This was not true, but this helped me feel angry and justified in that anger. This way, I did not have to face the fact that I was feeling lonely and insecure about being a new mom.

To be completely clear, it was my lack of vulnerability and my inability to relax that fueled these feelings. However, I was definitely not self-aware then. I had my first child in my early thirties, so I was not a young mom, but because I grew up in an extremely stressful and chaotic household, it was all I knew. Having my first child took me back to the trauma of growing up in that kind of environment, which I did not expect at all. Being a new mom brought with it all that old stress from when I was a child. I was used to having outlets for my needs, but now I had to ensure that I was taking care of my baby. I took my job as a new mother very seriously, and I also had the added pressure of doing things differently than my mom.

My husband and I decided to go to the couples' therapy workshop, along with other couples seeking help for their marriage and relationships, because I felt that we could learn how to communicate better as a couple. We found the Gottman Institute, which provided a research-based approach to relationships. It has been doing research on couples for forty years. I had read one of the books by Dr. John M. Gottman entitled, *The Seven Principles for Making Marriage Work*, and I had liked Dr. Gottman's methodology around marriage and relationships, so we were happy to attend a one-day couples' workshop.[13]

Thinking about these relationships always reminds me of my mom and how she didn't have the tools to deal with her stressors. She did not have a therapist or the Gottman Institute to learn proper coping and relationship skills. She was overworked and she had to deal with all the children in her household, so I can understand that she did not have a lot of time to sit down and chat with us. I understand that she was doing her best to keep us fed, have a roof over our heads, and clothes for us to go to school in. I understand all of this and I am grateful that I had all of this.

The funny thing was that when I started to feel completely overwhelmed with emotions related to my child and husband, I felt a kinship to my mom. I felt surges of energy through my body. I thought to myself that all these years in therapy had prepared me to face the pressures of being a mother in a new environment, but it was not that easy. After all, my mother had sixteen children and I only had one. I literally was baffled by that thought.

Clarity came to me, and with it came answers. I remember something Dr. Gottman said at the workshop that made me stop in my tracks. He said that women can be flooded with testosterone, just like men. That was what was happening to my mom: she would get flooded with testosterone, and she would lose it. The reason that I thought about my mom is because it was at these times that we would all run for cover. I had noticed I was getting flooded with the same hormone as my mother, and here Dr. Gottman was saying that women also get surges of testosterone. Bingo! *Okay, so this is what is happening to me,* I thought. When I was looking at my husband or getting overwhelmed by what I needed to do as a new mother, I was getting flooded with testosterone. What I needed to do was to cool it, chill out, and just breathe and relax.

This is why my mother had no problem having to defend her family, especially when it came to men. She would not back down; if a man was trying to hurt one of her sons, she would be ready to get into an altercation with them. Obviously, most men either think women will not fight them, or if a woman does not back down, they think she is crazy and they back down, because they know they are not dealing with a "normal" woman.

Well, that was my mother. These surges of testosterone explained why I was afraid that I would try to fight my husband. Neither my husband nor I believe in physical violence, so we did not believe in being physical with each other or with anyone else for that matter, so when I began experiencing these violent feelings, I called time out and we sought professional help. I thought to myself, *This feeling is just a feeling, just testosterone surging through my body, I do not have to act on it and it will settle down on its own; I just have to let it go through.*

It was so bizarre that Dr. Gottman addressed this and it helped me make sense of my mom's actions: how she was able to protect her children so fearlessly, but also unfortunately what she did to us when we were the receipient of all that testosterone.

Testosterone is normal and healthy, but it must be used with care, and it must also be respected. So now that I know I have tons of testosterone running through my body, I have to be fully aware of it. It can be misused, and I shouldn't use it with my husband and in my home, since it was not an appropriate time or place. I had to learn how to manage all this power and energy without using it in inappropriate ways.

The reason I tell you this story is because Dr. Gottman's explanation about excessive testosterone in women struck a chord with me. It helped put my situation in perspective. It pulled my husband out of the equation, where he should have not been in the first place. Blaming someone else when I did not know the answer to a problem was just my coping mechanism.

As I said, we had a wonderful time in our new environment, but I did not know how to breathe, meditate, or regulate both my cortisol and my testosterone levels. If I had had more self-awareness, I could have avoided some of the challenges I faced and could have kept both my cortisol and testosterone levels stabilized. Meditation would have made me feel better then, the way it makes me feel better now.

Self-awareness makes all the difference. If I know what is happening to me or what could happen, I can decide how I want to deal with it. The choices and feelings then become my decisions, and I can feel good about showing up with love, gentleness, and care for myself and others.

I still slip up every now and again, as we all do. When something happens to one of my children, for example, I tend to get very preoccupied with it. Time passes and I have other chores or projects I must work on, but the idea of whatever is happening with my child just does not go away and I go down a rabbit hole of worry, a rabbit hole of what-ifs. I get caught up looking down at the past and I explore the future, but then my present is nowhere in sight. Then I breathe, and this always helps.

How many of us get stuck in a loop of past-and-future thinking? It does not mean that we do not care about our children, because we do, but sometimes we believe that unless we are thinking about it over and over, we cannot solve the problem. I know this is especially true for me, as I like to think that if I fixate on something I can resolve whatever issue I'm having. This is where breathing meditations can be beneficial, because sometimes you must move on, get other chores or projects done, and then revisit what you would like to resolve with a family member later, when things are clearer for everyone.

When you get stuck, there are many ways to get away from the old records that play in your head and take up much of your time and attention. I personally follow the advice of Mel Robbins, who wrote a book called *The 5 Second Rule*.[14] The idea is that she gets herself out of a state of inaction by counting down from five; she says it is like a spaceship or a rocket that is going to be launched into outer space. It became a bestseller for a reason: it helped people break bad habits and encouraged them to give their brains a break.

I know that when we start something new, sometimes it is hard to move on to other tasks and put the thoughts of a current task away to let your brain work on it later. I am not a brain expert, but what I do know is that it is working even when you don't consciously focus on a problem to solve. Therefore, breathing is powerful in meditation because it allows you to be more thoughtful about the thoughts you want to have in the forefront of your mind.

It is a funny idea: be more thoughtful about the thoughts you have. It sounds redundant in its repetitive nature of circular thinking. But it holds some truth, because we have been told time and time again: watch your thoughts, watch what you put into your mind. Still, most of us do not listen. How do you watch your thoughts when you're being bombarded from every angle with deadlines, conversations, useless knowledge, other people's worries, and so much more? You have to be an information ninja to escape all those ideas, thoughts, and distractions that are being shot your way.

I listened to Jack Canfield's tape a long time ago titled *Self-esteem & Peak Performance*.[15] There were so many great stories and examples, but there was one in particular that I found fascinating. He talked about how whatever we learn, whatever we think about, we then find in the world. For example, Jack Canfield was talking to his wife about how he had learned a new word. He told his wife something like: "Hey, I just learned this new word, and it just happened to be up on a billboard, can you believe that?" His wife answered, "That sign has been there for twenty years." I took this to mean that unless you look more in depth, unless you're looking for something specific, you might not be able to find it. But once you recognize and internalize it, you see it everywhere.

> *Do you not owe it to yourself to find true happiness?*

This ability also means that by doing the breathing exercises, you can get rid of thoughts and ideas that no longer serve you or that put you on a roller coaster of turmoil and dysfunction. If you are doing or thinking something that is no longer helping you and is causing you stress, taking up your precious time for no real reason other than to make your life more difficult, you can break that habit by being more mindful.

Also, if you think about it, who is going to prioritize your happiness if not you? Sure, there can be lots of loving and caring people around you who only want the best for you, but do you not owe it to yourself to find true happiness?

Sometimes when you want to change and grow, your

lower brain is still trying to hold on to how things are, more out of habit than real need. Therefore, meditation is so important because you can make an informed decision on what is actually needed versus following an unnecessary habit. Just as the great oak tree must grow, we all must continue to grow, because we are alive, it is exciting, and it brings our souls great happiness. Always remember, one person's understanding of growth is very different than another person's, and getting connected to yourself through breathing meditation will help you sort it out.

When we form habits, it feels easier to keep them than to make a change. I know that for myself, breaking the habit is going to be difficult, and the path of least resistance always seems better. The problem is that we know deep down inside that growth is inevitable. We can deny it, but we eventually must admit what we are doing.

If you did something and it helped you in one environment but now you are in a different environment and that thing that helped you before is now causing you pain, why would you want to hold onto it? I struggle with trying to make the best choices for myself and my environment, meaning my family, my physical, mental, and spiritual health, and other aspects of myself.

I love the growth that I have achieved, and I love where I have taken myself, but it has not been without getting to know myself better; it has not been without getting to shed pretense and deal with different problems and feelings I hadn't been able to wrestle with before. I still struggle with some other very intricate ideas and my lower brain does not want to let go. I have been so wrapped around a certain way of life, of making my world safe and livable, and now that I am completely happy, I want to say goodbye to those feelings.

WHEN I WAS YOUNGER it was hard to have my own space, so I knew that I wanted that for my future. I liked being part of a big family, but having so many people around you all the time can get tiresome. The house was full of so many people with so many different needs. In my mind, I always had an idea of what I had to do.

I knew that I had to get a good education so I would get a good job, and then I could afford to have my own space where I could take care of all my needs. When you have had so much trauma as a child from living in chaos, it is hard to feel safe in your own skin—not because you literally are not safe in your own skin, but because all of the interactions and all of the feelings you have when you live in a household with so many people seem normal, so you cannot understand that you can live any other way.

Meditation then gives you the space to change all of the ideas and feelings that are no longer true or useful. Giving yourself space through breathing helps you change

Giving yourself space through breathing helps you change the programming in your mind and body.

the programming in your mind and body.

Remember that I did not learn about meditation until I was much older. When my life settled down, I graduated from college, and had a good job, I then had time to heal from my childhood challenges. I actually started going to therapy at the age of eighteen and then continued for the rest of my life. I not only did therapy to help me heal, forgive, and move on from my past, but it also helped me develop emotionally.

Creating space is where therapy helped me and, later on, where meditating and breathing helped me achieve more. Breathing gives you the space to allow the wounded parts of you to heal and move on. Some of that work is hard, but with a simple meditation practice you can start getting to the root of anything you want to learn or change. I had to do a lot of digging and decluttering in my life: a process I call "shedding what no longer works for you."

When I was eighteen years old, I started talking to some of my friends about some of the hurt and sadness that I had endured as a child. I had never shared any of my feelings with anyone before, but I thought it was time.

Although my friends were trying to be loving and caring, they definitely were a little overwhelmed by having to hear my stories. Afterward I felt uncomfortable, both for myself and for my friends. I didn't want to share this information with them, because they were not professional therapists, and I thought, *Why should I burden them with things they cannot change or help me with?*

It was at that time that I decided I needed to be able

to talk to someone who could listen to my stories. I needed someone who could listen to me and would not make me feel awkward. Growing up in a dysfunctional environment definitely makes one feel awkward. I had to talk to a professional who could give me the safe space to talk about what I needed to talk about, and then I could move on with my life.

I went to my first therapy session. I felt weird, awkward, and uncomfortable, but I knew it was better than trying to have my friends understand what I was talking about. I needed a therapist to help me sort through my stories and my feelings around them. I needed to share my experience with someone who could give me the space and listen to my story. My first therapist and I were a good match, because we both felt safe and comfortable with each other when we started working together.

It was the first time in my life I could talk freely about what happened in my home, what feelings I had, and how I saw the world. I was able to talk about my confusion and my feelings about stuff that happened. It was so refreshing to have someone listen to me and validate my feelings. This helped me so much, because I no longer had to walk around with the lingering confusion I had when I was growing up. I was not crazy, and although my family may have had different views than me, it did not mean that how I saw things was incorrect. I totally needed that reality check.

When you grow up in a household with particular realities, you could be misguided, but I did not always agree with the actions my family took. For the therapist to let me set the scene, explain it, and ask me questions so she could be clear about what I was saying, helped me gain perspective and feel more at ease.

I never questioned or wondered too much when growing up, but once I left my home at eighteen, I felt safe enough to start asking questions and trying to make sense of things. These things, which I did not have time to tease apart, would show up again and again until I sorted through them. If I tried to brush them under the rug, they would resurface. Then I would have to deal with them.

For me, meditation has been a window to a sense of self. When I was growing up, we were a pack of people who were there to love, care, and help each other out in our own ways. As I said, being a child in this type of environment, with a whole social system already built in, comes with its own restrictions and norms. For me to be myself, by myself, was not frowned upon, but it was not something that was commonly practiced in our family. We always had someone we could be with, whether it was a sibling, parent, or grandparent. I appreciated having this level of time and love from my family, but it could get a little difficult for me. Sometimes I wanted time to think about things on my own. What was most difficult is that I did not agree with many of the ideas or methods my family members preferred, but when I was with them I did not question them, because asking questions made them feel attacked.

I wanted some space to think of nothing. I often think

about what meditation could have helped me with as a child. For one thing, I could have had the opportunity to have deeper conversations with my family. We were always so busy doing something that we did not have the time to settle down or learn more about each other. It would have been nice to have clear ideas of what I really liked, what made me laugh, what I thought about certain events, or even what was going on outside the walls of our home—to get a better feel for my siblings and what was going on with them. Most of the time I was not talked to as I scurried from here to there, and anything I learned about our family came from listening to others talking. Now that I write this, it all appears so typical; yes, many families operate in this way. If this is so normal, why would meditation have helped me?

First, I would only hear gossip about events or people from my family. I did not receive information firsthand. If I had meditated, I could have been much better at having conversations with others. Overall, I did an okay job as the youngest child trying to understand all my siblings. I tried to have conversations with them, but it was actually hard to do this with my family members, because no one really talked about anything; we just did stuff together.

My relationship with my grandfather would have been richer had I known about meditation. I truly loved my grandfather. When I was growing up, he was one person who made some sense to me. He had his routines, and he also showed me kindness when I had an especially rough day.

He and I would go shopping when I was little. We always left the house at five or six o'clock in the morning, either on a Saturday or Sunday. I always loved to get up so early in the morning and go search for books with him. We'd explore yard sales or go to a swap meet, depending on what my grandfather wanted to do. This is the way it worked: Grandpa would say *Hey, I'm going to the flea market tomorrow to look for some books; do you want to come along?* and when I said yes he would just wake me up early in the morning by gently pushing my head a couple of times until I woke up; he was always already dressed and ready to go. When I opened my eyes, he would just nod and I would jump out of bed. Soon after, we were off to a swap meet or yard sales in search of the week's reading purchases.

If I'd known how to meditate, my relationship with my grandfather would have been more complete; I would have been able to have more conversations with him when we spent time together book shopping on the weekends. I would have had the space to talk to him more about his life, giving him the time to share his life stories with me through our conversations so I could in turn pass them down to my children. They could have given me experience and clarity.

MY SISTER, WHO WAS BORN right before me, was supposed to be the last child. She was going to be a twin, so my parents would have had fifteen children. Long story short, my mother's pregnancy with my sister was a difficult one. She almost lost both twins. My sister was born prematurely and was therefore saved, but sadly her twin did not make it. Despite this difficulty, she grew up to be a healthy adult.

Then I was born soon after, and then my mother adopted my youngest brother. Now we were sixteen children in total. All my siblings liked to do different activities together. In such a large family, the kids are usually left on their own, and the older siblings usually call the shots for what games, activities, or events the younger kids are going to do. I was just happy to be invited, excited to be part of the team.

My family called me "grandma" when I was young because I used to act like one—probably because I did not quite go with the flow, and I would put on the brakes for some of the activities. Or maybe it was because I was a tattletale; if something looked dangerous, I was telling my mother. In fact, I told my mother just about everything. This was an interesting situation for a child to be in and also a very lonely one, because your siblings think twice before they invite you to play with them.

Through meditation I have been able to allow some of these needs that I had as a child to leave me as an adult, because they no longer serve me. I had to unlearn that behavior and tell myself that I am no longer a little kid; I can take care of myself and ensure that I am safe, happy, and healthy. As a child, I did not have access to all that, but as an adult I do.

Meditation has allowed me to separate myself from

things that are not my concern. We can definitely outgrow these habits that we learn when we are young. Sometimes when you have a deep and ingrained habit, it appears almost impossible to get rid of. However, anything is possible, and through meditation I am able to feel any old feelings, hold them up to the light, and see if they are something that is relevant to me and something I want to spend time on, or something that I must let go.

Meditation has helped me sort through so many different feelings and emotions that I had pushed down when I did not know what to do with them. Now I no longer have to avoid them, and this has helped me change habits and actions that did not make my life enjoyable. For example, thinking that I had to fix everything and help everyone around me constantly was insane, but some how this is what I learned as a child. This is why I would project my feelings or insecurities on others, when in reality I had no idea I was doing this. It was such an external and completely misguided way to live. Therefore, I am writing this book because breathing meditation is now a habit for me; it is now a part of me. Meditation and focusing on my breathing helps me relax, and it helps me get in touch with what I am feeling, which in turn helps me get in touch with what I am thinking. I wanted to have this so I could fully show up, so I could be as happy as possible and finally understand that happiness is an inside job. Breathing meditation helps you get that inside job done. Getting there is not easy, because some of those old habits are persistent little energy fields, but it does not mean that we cannot grow beyond them.

Hands down, the biggest benefit of breathing meditation is unconditional self-love. I am listening to an audiobook by Laura Berman called *Quantum Love.*[16] I started listening to it after I had seen a therapist who recommended that I do some energy work as the next form of self-development. What I found is that she is basically saying the same thing: people need to go back to their home, which is their heart—their unconditional self-love. When you go back home to your heart, you can learn to love others unconditionally, and it starts with loving yourself.

The thread that I have been running into in all the work I do in becoming happier, healthier, more successful, and more satisfied in my life boils down to self-love. Everyone should start with uncondional self-love, and then everything will fall into line.

Why would unconditional self-love be so important? Because it is your ultimate happiness meter. If you have unconditional self-love, you will always be okay. Your decisions will be yours; you will be kind, gentle, and loving with yourself always, and when you do this, you will save years of heartache and insecurity by doing what you are meant to do here in this lifetime, which is to be truly, utterly, and unequivocally happy.

> *Start with uncondional self-love, and then everything will fall into line.*

Let us think about this for a moment. Anything that happens in your life is okay—anything. Why? First, you do not abandon yourself ever, because you are always there for yourself, and second, you are always on the right track. This means that even if you must make hard decisions, even if some challenging events happen in your life, you are going to be okay because you will not be unnecessarily harsh with yourself and you will always look at yourself through a loving lens.

You will always show up for yourself; you will make yourself smile, laugh, and giggle. You will be a model of unconditional self-love for yourself, and guess what that unconditionally self-loving person does for others? They love others, because they do not judge them; why should they, when they do not judge themselves? You cannot give to others what you do not have. You cannot give to others what you do not practice yourself.

You cannot give to others what you do not practice yourself.

So, if you are giving yourself unconditional self-love, you have more unconditional love to give.

And who, I ask, does not need unconditional love? Well, we can all appreciate it because unconditional love helps us show up as who we are, with no stupid judgment. And anyway, who started judging others as not good enough, not smart enough, or other negative things?

It really sucks to hear that people are meant to feel bad just because they are themselves. We are all absolutely phenomenal individuals, each and every one of us, but we just get confused and we lose our way. When you find your way back home to your unconditional self-love, you have found the most beautiful place in the world; the best place that has ever existed or will ever exist. Breathing is just the first step. Happy travels, my friend!

MEDITATION

BECAUSE THIS CHAPTER is about hormones, we are going to incorporate a method of breathing that will quickly allow you to relax and regulate the hormones that are running through your body.

Instead of breathing in and out silently, you will be breathing out a vibrational sound. Doing this privately, away from others, will allow you to be as loud as you need to be.

Take a deep breath in, then when you breathe out, you will activate a vibration to immediately tell your body to relax. Sometimes it takes ten of these to get you where you need to be.

Breathe out any one of the following words while trying to vibrate them while you breathe out:

> *"Aaauuugggghhhh"*
> *"Lllllaaannnnggg"*
> *"Ooommmmmmm"*

What is important is that your body feels the vibration as you exhale, which will immediately tell it to relax and will allow whatever hormone is running through your body to also relax. Usually you will get an immediate yawn when you do this, and your muscles will loosen.

QUESTIONS

- Has stress ever negatively affected your relationships? How so?
- Are you a perfectionist? Do you feel you need to be in control all the time?
- How has your childhood affected the way you respond to stress or conflict?

05
REST AND DIGEST

"At the center of your garden lies a golden fountain. This fountain represents the flow of positive, empowering thoughts that drive your actions and emotions and manifest as your outer circumstances. With careful maintenance and irrigation, this fountain can become a crystal-clear beacon of beauty and peace that nurtures every component of your life. In order to achieve this harmonious flow, we have to rebuild our thinking from the ground up. We call this process cognitive restructuring."

—Dr. Cheyenne Bryant, *Mental Detox*[17]

I was in awe of peaceful and happy people when I was young. *Look at how they laugh and how they carry themselves around, look at how curious they are*, I thought. This was wonderful energy to be around, and I wanted this for myself so badly. I wanted to have conversations that were interesting to me. I wanted to learn, have fun, and simply enjoy this wonderful world.

I liked hanging out with my grandfather because he loved to read, take walks, and garden like I did. He had a calm, trusting, and loving energy that I appreciated in my home. I loved that he gave me that sanctuary in a chaotic house.

IF YOU NEVER LEARNED how to rest and digest, then you never learned that first, rest is your right, and second, you are a human being who needs to give yourself much-needed love and care. When I was growing up, my mom tried to instill this in me; she was always so hard on herself and could not find the time or motivation to take a proper rest, so I think she tried her best to encourage me to do so.

When we think of stress and its impact on the sympathetic nervous system, the toll that it takes on our bodies and our health, it becomes extremely problematic for us. The best way I found to shift from a constant fight-or-flight state to a rest-and-digest state was through breathing and meditation. When we rest and digest, we allow our bodies and brains to take a break, we allow more positivity to enter, and we feel better as a result.

We need to cultivate the positive thoughts that energize us.

What are some of the challenges we face when trying to reach rest-and-digest? For one, many of us don't know about it as children. If your mother does not know how to properly rest and digest, then you think that being in fight-or-flight all the time is the right way to be. However, your body and mind do not agree with this, because they manifest your stress as migraines or other ailments.

When we become aware of our habits and thoughts, we realize that just because we're not worrying or stressing about something doesn't mean something will go wrong. It sounds so illogical, but these are the thoughts that go through our minds, and we're often unaware of them. These thoughts are what make our breathing shallow, that don't allow us to relax our nervous systems. We need to cultivate the positive thoughts that energize us, rather than a negative and perfectionist mindset that hinders us in the long run.

THE FIRST TIME REST-AND-DIGEST was solidly introduced to me, I was at a dinner party with my family, along with several other family friends. This one was a little different, however; we would be learning how to cook a few recipes from a five-star chef, and after the cooking portion of the evening, we would enjoy the food. Although I would not consider myself a cook, the dinner was delicious.

While we were eating, one of the mothers mentioned that she liked to take a break before she had her dessert. She said that she and her husband liked to "rest and digest." The way she explained it was that she liked to allow her body to relax and digest the food. Then, later on in the evening, she would enjoy some dessert.

I thought this was a fascinating idea. I usually have my meal followed by dessert almost right away, but I felt that her method of resting between courses was very good. It would allow the body to not only digest what had already been eaten, but more importantly, it would allow it time to be ready for the next course, which was often my favorite part.

Giving your body a break, giving yourself a break, and giving everyone else around you a break: what a concept! It sounded like a foolproof idea. A few weeks later, I had the chance to do some research on what rest-and-digest meant. When reading the definition, I remembered hearing the term from someone else in a different context; a rehabilitation trainer I had worked with a few months prior had also mentioned the term to me, but framed in a different way.

When I started working with this personal trainer, I noticed that he was wearing beads on his wrist. When I asked him about them, he said that he wore them as a reminder to himself to rest and digest. When I asked him what he meant, he said that when he got too distracted or busy, the beads helped bring him back to the present, to be more intentional in his actions.

He said, "When you are in rest-and-digest, you actually are allowing your body to relax and to rebuild itself. It's like you are getting a good night's rest. Because you are in rest-and-digest, your body is relaxed and all the systems in your body work better." In that moment I was more focused on the beads than the rest-and-digest bit, so it didn't come to mind again until that dinner party weeks later.

When my friend mentioned it at the dinner, my interest definitely peaked. To rest and digest is to literally take a break; it means to allow your body down time so it can allow your system to reset itself. When the body is in fight-or-flight, all non-emergency systems shut down. However, when you are in rest-and-digest mode, your body is not coursing with cortisol. As the name suggests, your body is taking a break, and you are relaxed. It is important to relax, because this helps your system regulate itself. It helps you make decisions with greater ease and with better results. A clear mind always makes better decisions.

A clear mind always makes better decisions.

Unfortunately, if you are not facing real, physical threats and you are still constantly in fight-or-flight mode, then you are basically creating cortisol for no good reason, and in a way it causes your body harm. The high levels of cortisol tweak your nervous system in ways that become extremely problematic. This is especially troublesome when you are simply trying to go through your days as a regular person, a person who doesn't face real threats at every corner.

Too much of anything is not a good thing. Like everything else in the world, some cortisol is okay, but too much can have short-term and long-lasting negative impacts.

When you breathe in an organized manner, which is usually longer breaths out than in, you put your body in the rest-and-digest phase, which means that you are giving much-needed attention and love to yourself.

It is easy for most of us to be stressed about something and not even know it; we go from one thing to another to another, and we forget to take good care of ourselves. We have been taught to prioritize the success of others and our groups over ourselves. These messages are prevalent in many societies, but just because they are well-worn does not mean that we cannot change them and take care of ourselves.

There are countless thick, defining books out there that have tons of research and theories about the psychology of human beings. Ideas and habits are formed through brain structure, custom, or in religious practice. The idea of rest-and-digest for the individual then would be a state of putting your body's nervous system into alignment, but many societies fail to teach us this, so now it is our turn to learn this on our own for the sake of our health.

But where is the information about the medicinal value of rest-and-digest in our world? A simple concept is not all that helpful if it is buried under research or a whole slew of information. You will definitely feel the negative effects of keeping your mind active and stressed for long periods of time. I know that when I took the time to meditate, it brought me relief. Therefore, if you do not put the right amount of time into your self-care and rest, then those negative consequences will come back to haunt you later. Better to be preventative. We are all trying our best, and the breathing meditation work will get you to the place you want to be.

THE IDEA OF REST-AND-DIGEST is to oppose fight-or-flight, and it would have been nice for someone to have explained this to me in my twenty years of therapy. Or maybe I was told, but I just wasn't ready to hear and incorporate it into my life.

Meditation breathing and this concept of rest-and-digest are two sides of the same coin. When you do meditation breathing, you are literally putting your body into rest-and-digest mode. You are giving your whole system a break, and this is extremely good for your whole mind, body, and soul.

Many people in my life do not know about rest-and-digest, and it can become a complicated concept to understand, depending on whom you ask. My hope is to make it as accessible and simple as possible to you so you can use it at any time: maybe daily, weekly, or even monthly.

Anytime you do this is a positive. You will be surprised at how your body rewards you. My health has improved, not in small part by not feeling stressed out all the time and chugging coffee. I am able to feel more confident and relaxed with life in general, and I think this has all contributed to my overall health improving.

When we are in a fight-or-flight frame of mind, even if we are not aware of it, we can feel uncomfortable, fearful, sad, depressed, angry, or upset. We walk around with a sort of challenge hanging over our head, and we cannot figure out what it is. We then try to do what we can to live our lives and get through our days as best we can. Some of us do better than others, and if you are doing any self-care on a regular basis, then you may be too far advanced for this book, and I say good for you for taking care of yourself.

However, if you do not feel like you have the time or the luxury for self-care, then this is your chance to take this meditation practice more seriously. You see, I am writing this book because I have been on this journey all my life; I have reached better personal platforms, but there has been a lot of cleaning up to do. When we are kids, we do not have control of our environment. We respect, believe in, and trust our caretakers, as we do not know any different.

When we are taken care of well, we could still have some of our own challenges (no one is completely free from hardship); people think some challenges are harder than others, but I would have to say all challenges are challenges. This is part of being free and being able to inspire and build a happy life for yourself.

I had read about people turning on or off, depending on the situation. This means that they were going all day (on) and then at night, they would unplug (off) and do it all again the next day. Back then, when I heard these stories, I thought, *Wow, that sounds so great! This person knows exactly what is going on with them and how they operate.*

Those are misguided thoughts, however, because it is not good for their health to be in fight-or-flight all day long. Now I think that is a tough way to live, because you never get to take a little time for yourself during the day; you must continue to go until you can't go anymore, and then you sleep.

MY FAMILY AND I once went skiing. I did not put my long-distance training on pause for these vacations, so I had run twenty miles the day before. My kids were having skiing lessons, and I believed I had to be out there with them. My body was protesting pretty badly, but I ignored it. This was obviously before I learned to rest and digest. It was fairly icy that day, and I could barely walk. Inevitably, not long after I started to ski down this very icy slope, I lost control and ended up flipping over, hitting my head on the ground, and landing with skis facing opposite directions. Ouch! I was stuck in the snow and called out to my husband who was in front of me, and he trekked back up to free me from my skis. I thought I was fine, that I had just twinged my knees a bit. I moved to get up, but just then I saw a lady skiing toward me quickly with her daughter, and she was yelling "No!" emphatically. But it was too late; I attempted to stand up.

Not surprisingly, I fell back down to the ground. Her daughter, who was probably seven, looked at me with terror in her eyes, and when I saw how scared she was for me, I tried to play the pain down. I think I actually managed to smile at her to reassure her that I was fine, that it wasn't really that big of a deal, that I do this type of stuff all the time. Not, not, and not. It was a big deal, and I was in a lot of pain, but I did not want to traumatize the little kid.

I assured the mom I would not try to get up again and that I would get someone to take me off the slope. With that, she and her daughter turned around and went back to the other side of the slope where they had been skiing.

I was actually happy she came over to try to lend a hand and ensure that I was safe.

When I had tried to get up, I felt that my bones were rubbing up and through each other, so I knew I would not be walking anywhere anytime soon. My husband got the medics, and I was carried off the hill on a stretcher; I could feel that my knee got the bulk of the damage. I waited in the car while my husband got the kids, and then we drove to the emergency room. I learned I had torn my knee and had a lot of swelling around my injuries. I could not walk, and this put an immediate and real halt on my training program. If I wanted to continue training for long-distance endurance sports, I would have to get surgery.

Since I couldn't really do much about the situation, I was pretty much forced to take it easy. A friend of mine visited me when I was injured and told me a story of one of their friends and how this person had a bad accident just as I did. She said that while their body recovered, they did not recover psychologically from the accident. I wondered what that meant.

To relax, I didn't revert to the strategies I learned at Berkeley. Instead, I started to journal and write some poetry, whatever came to mind. My friend was trying to get me to go to therapy, because she knew I used sports to decompress, as a way to deal with my stress. Since I would not be doing any sports for a while, I would need other coping strategies. This was not bad advice, so I found a therapist and let them know I was ordered to rest because of a very serious injury, but that I had been training for a very long run. The therapist asked me what I was running from.

I found this both humorous and uncomfortable. I think the discomfort was because they were asking me to think about my life and why I did things. For someone with my upbringing, with fifteen siblings and using sports as my way to get into a flow or clear my mind, I did not know how to rest and digest without sports.

When I thought about it, most of my life, if not all my life, I have been moving in this world through bursts of cortisol. Maybe some people are more prone to fight or flight, while some people truly know how to rest and digest, but even if some are predisposed to be more stressed or anxious than others, I am here to tell you that if I could figure out how to do it, so can you. When you meditate and learn about your breath, you can get yourself, your brain, and every cell in your body to rest and digest and get off that cortisol wave. Cortisol is an important hormone; it does not matter who you are, some cortisol is extremely important. It is when you overproduce cortisol that things get unbalanced. A common story of this happening is when people get "super strength" and accomplish lifesaving feats. The reason your body does not do that regularly is because when you get to these situations, they are usually life or death.

THERE ARE ALSO THINGS we can do to reach this state. For example, if we are getting good sleep, this can lower our cortisol. If we are exercising, this can also lower our cortisol and put us in rest-and-digest. Dr. Rangan Chatterjee, in his book *How to Make Disease Disappear,* has some great recipes to help your brain. How much work our bodies and minds are doing also relies on our nutrition. For example, with Dr. Chatterjee's smoothies, you can literally help your brain think and work better, which in turn makes you feel better.

I have also listened to the advice of author and writer Abraham Hicks, who has several videos on her YouTube channel. Something that stuck with me is when she stated that disease is when you are dis-eased.[18] Therefore, if we are at ease or in a rest-and-digest frame of mind, this can literally help our health. It sounds too good to be true. Make yourself happy and watch your dis-ease disappear. Watch your rest-and-digest, and your life, get better.

Julia Ross, MA, the author of both *The Mood Cure* and *The Diet Cure,* also talks at length about different hormones and explains how to naturally help your body and mind work with the foods you eat.[19]

She references the studies she has done with her patients on how certain nutrients affect your body. However, the scientific jargon is not what I am here to teach you; I am just here to tell you that when you begin to meditate and listen to your breathing, your life will change. I know it is life transforming. Your breath is life; you are life.

Again, the scope of this book is not to get you one hundred percent healthy, because that truly is an individual journey, and each person is different. My only goal, and I will continue to repeat it throughout the book, is to get you to learn how to meditate and see how wonderful it makes your life. I do not proclaim to have all the answers; all I can share with you is what I have learned through my own experience as I continue to develop myself into the best, healthiest self I can be. And my experience has told me that breathing as a way to get to a state of rest-and-digest is a practical and real tool to help us heal our bodies from cortisol and get to healing.

We should not be in fight-or-flight mode all the time, since this is like having your car going one hundred miles per hour all day long and even at night while you sleep. This is not giving your body or mind a break. I have heard of people who drink lots of caffeinated drinks in the morning and throughout the day, and then need to take a sleep aid, natural or otherwise, to try to get some sleep. How long before this system does not work anymore? This is where rest-and-digest comes in; it is designed to give you breaks throughout the day, so you do not have to rely on so much caffeine and other external substances to get you through.

It is about having access to both the fight-or-flight mode and the rest-and-digest mode. Think about saving or preserving energy so you can be happy, healthy, and successful every day of your life. You are not going to feel one hundred percent great every single day—none of us can ever do that—but your life has the potential to be great most of the time.

Some of us are so wired up that we think we are unstoppable, but deep down inside, we know it is all just this great big façade and we are not coping well. I was not born with this knowledge, I had to learn it like everyone else.

I grew up in a household where we did not subscribe to that rest-and-digest idea. Man, that would have been nice! I see people who are happy, healthy, and successful every day, which means they have that rest-and-digest routine down, maybe even from childhood.

There are millions of people out there who grew up in households where you had to work incredibly hard. My household had a single mom with sixteen kids, and that was hard because my mom had to be both mom and dad; she did not get a break. This in turn taught us not to take breaks, either. She would walk around the house, and if you were lounging around, she considered it a crime. It did not make sense to us, but if you wanted to rest, you actually had to do it away from Mom, because if she saw you resting then she would make you do something, anything. Sometimes I would even try to take naps in the sun-hot car, because she was that adamant about keeping busy.

There can be arguments both for and against taking breaks, but what I am trying to give you is some information on its benefits. You need to rest and digest to have happiness, health, and success. If you do not, it is near impossible to have these wonderful things in your life.

The most efficient way to take this break is to meditate. You do not necessarily have to be eating or have eaten to rest and digest. I think the term has more to do with the state of rest than it has to do with digestion, more to do with the mindset. When I learned about rest-and-digest and truly started taking it seriously, I learned I could show up however I wanted to.

The fake-it-till-you-make-it mindset can be helpful, but it is not sustainable in the long run. The truth is, you must be honest with yourself to truly provide a real rest-and-digest environment within. It is medicinal to your mind and body because it is allowing you to truly stop, take care of yourself, and allow yourself to feel safe, loved, and cared for. Some people have no knowledge of these practices because they are surrounded by people who are not familiar with basic self-care concepts or, like my mother, do not have the time or bandwidth to take on yet another item on their to-do list.

It is very unfortunate, but it is what it is. I think that the way my mom rested and digested was with caffeine, and her complete relaxation was done by praying. The latter, some say, is equivalent to meditating; praying, chanting, and similar practices can be your rest-and-digest framework, so really that was Mom's way of reaching to the things she was familiar with to calm her mind. Not to say my mother had her rest-and-digest system down, even though she regularly prayed. No matter how relaxed she seemed at any given moment, fight or flight was always just underneath the surface, waiting to take over.

It is what I would characterize as post-traumatic stress. I do not recall any specific stories, but I do remember her telling me she had to take on a lot, what with her sixteen kids and the pressure to protect us from the outside world. She told me how that was a challenge she took on proudly as a mother. I completely respected her for that, but I was also frustrated and a bit sad for her, having to deal with all the pressure and trauma of having to be everything to all us children. Our family was its own village, literally. She had to be "on" all the time.

WHEN I THINK OF REST-AND-DIGEST with regard to my mother and anyone else who has a hectic life, I feel it is a hard and exhausting way to live. Losing my mother in 2016 devastated me, so I have been reflecting deeply about her role in my life and how my experiences differ from hers. Moving through this world without her, I feel so much more determined to find my space to rest and digest.

Now then, how did I get the time to take care of myself? I was always searching for peace and calm; despite my upbringing, I knew that I could live a more peaceful life outside of my mother's home.

First, I planned. I decided at an early age that I would work toward having a more peaceful and tranquil environment when I grew up. I wanted to put myself in a situation where I could be safe, happy, healthy, and successful.

Next, I would notice others who embodied the life I wanted to have. On the outside, it may have looked like I was already in this calm and tranquil environment, but I had to do a lot of meditating and breathing to get my insides to match my outsides.

I began getting the success, education, jobs, and relationships in order, but what I was missing was self-love and true happiness, internal happiness. During my journey, one of the biggest things I learned is to never compare yourself to others, because they are only ever showing you the surface level, not what they are feeling inside.

MEDITATION

THIS MEDITATION AND BREATHING exercise is useful when you have had a long day and you want to do a refresh-and-reset without consuming sugar or caffeine.

You will need a bed or chair you can sit in for five to ten minutes. A quiet place is preferable, but it is not necessary to get the same results. With this exercise, your breathing is soft, and your main goal is to count in your mind. Simply lie down for five to ten minutes. If you will be doing a five-minute rest, you should count to thirty ten times. If you are doing a ten-minute rest, you should count to thirty twenty times. After this you can get up, and you should feel extremely clear-minded and refreshed.

QUESTIONS

- In what ways do you relieve your stress?
- Do you ever rest and digest after a meal or a busy day?
- How often do you find yourself 'riding the cortisol wave'?

06
CLARITY

"What are these tiny steps that we make every day? They're habits. And humans truly are, as it's often said, creatures of habit. Research suggests that almost half of all the activities we engage in over the course of a single day are done out of habit. Does anyone need to tell you to brush your teeth? Close your front door? Make a cup of coffee in the morning? Of course not. You carry out these little acts without thinking. But such routines can be incredibly powerful. Small regular habits hold far more sway over our health than large and occasional activities."

—Dr Rangan Chatterjee, *Feel Better in 5*[20]

"Most people think they lack motivation when they really lack clarity."

—James Clear[21]

I was a freshman in high school when my sister told me I planned too much, which was a stunning criticism to me. This was around the time that someone had given me a copy of the book by Napoleon Hill, *Think and Grow Rich*, and I was extremely fascinated by the idea that we could literally decide how we want to live our lives by what we focus on.[22]

From my understanding of the book, he was saying this: *You can ask of life whatever you want and life will willingly pay, but once you have set the task, you have to be ready for the results.* I felt a little self-conscious about my planning after my sister interrogated me. However, the planning is fun, and for the most part, it gives me pretty good results.

There came a time when I started looking at others to see what I wanted for my future. My ideas changed as I grew older, but one thing that stayed consistent for me was the importance of creating long-term goals; this was one habit I had down. I didn't have to iron out all the details straight away, I just made three- and five-year plans.

However I arrived at the goal was not carved in stone, so I could be as creative and flexible as I needed to reach my destination. One thing that I did learn was to start to cultivate habits that would directly impact my goals. These habits literally changed the trajectory of my life.

Let's go back to people who have this figured out, who are happy, healthy, and satisfied. These people do breath work and meditation. When you meditate, you automatically get clarity. Clarity gives you happiness. Clarity gives you clear direction. Clarity gives you energy and efficiency. Therefore, if breathing exercise and meditation give you clarity, then we need to protect our meditation and breathing practice, because this will help us create and maintain useful habits.

Your body sometimes sends certain messages to your brain that are not useful to you, and if you want to do things differently, you have to override these messages.

For example, let's say that you are trying to work on a project and you are moving along just fine, and then you begin to get derailed, taking away your concentration on the project at hand. The way you override these is by taking a break and just breathing. Do ten to twenty breaths, and then relax and get back to focusing on what you are doing.

Maybe you need to drink some water, or maybe you need to drink one of Dr. Chatterjee's smoothies for your brain to have the energy to focus on your project.

Is this what I want, or is this just a habit? Is it serving my highest needs and wants?

You have to approach yourself at the level of what you need next. This habit of breathing then can be your guide to your energy stores and can help you with anything you have to get done.

Someone who is self-aware and has been practicing intentional living will likely be able to get a true reading on what they are feeling and what is happening. What that means is that to get there, you have to say to yourself: *Is this what I want, or is this just a habit? Is it serving my highest needs and wants?*

I know the questions seem simple, and even then we think it's too much work. This stuff is not easy, but I can tell you, getting that clarity is worth it. Your sanity, health, joy, and happiness are completely worth it.

Clarity helps you get rid of habits that you no longer need. Breathing and meditating help you sort out your mind and your life by offering you the space to clear up clutter, get rid of what is not working, and create the habits that you just haven't found the time to cultivate. How do you want to live your life? Breathe and meditate to clear your mind and get the clarity that will transform your life.

Think about it: if we live from a place of default and confusion, it leaves us restless and tired. You are not going to get a different result than the one you want if you are not doing the right things.

As I write this, it seems so simple, but how many of us want something but then do the opposite of what we want, and then get upset we didn't get the desired outcome? Maybe we self-sabotage, maybe we're afraid of success. Why do we say we want something and then do something else? We might sabotage our happiness because subconsciously we think we don't deserve to be happy.

When I was working with my therapist about five years ago, I told her I felt guilty if I was happy. I said I have no idea why this was, but I just felt guilty. She told me, "I want you to repeat this affirmation regularly to yourself to override the messaging that makes you feel uncomfortable when you want to feel happy: 'It is safe for me to be happy.'"

Drop the mic.

This was so weird, but I did it—and it worked! I guess growing up with so many siblings and a mother who was overworked and tired all the time meant that everyone was broadcasting a very specific message: life is hard, we have to work hard, and there is no time to be happy. I was "spoiled" if I thought that I wanted to be happy while others were suffering in this world. I thought I was spoiled and ungrateful if I thought that I could possibly want to be happy. Even if not stated explicitly, that was what my upbringing taught me about happiness.

I JUST COMPLETED my first Ironman event in Oregon, and I found myself smiling while out on the course. It was extremely tough and painful at times, but I could still muster up a smile. I love to smile because it makes your body feel good and it allows you to relax. Smiling makes me breathe and meditate while doing endurance sports, and I repeat to myself: "It is safe for me to be happy!" Sure, the Ironman kicked my ass, but I also kicked its ass, and we were happy, kicking each other's asses.

That is life. Whatever you want in your life, whatever works for you, figure it out and enjoy it. I did not think I could actually do it, but my therapist helped me realize I could. I can be happy with whatever it is I am doing, and I love that.

When you figure out what makes you happy and you fully embrace it, you save yourself tons of energy. Not only that, but you use your time in ways that you enjoy, which makes a world of difference.

When you don't give yourself permission to breathe and meditate, the patchwork you put on your soul is like putting a bandage on a leaky pipe versus just replacing it and avoiding the struggle in the long term. You are literally using a ton of energy, time and time again, to put basically useless bandages on your problem, and meanwhile you're still wasting tons of water and the bill will be enormous: a temporary, expensive, and damaging "fix."

Clarity is extremely powerful, because not only is it good for your health, but it also allows you to incorporate the habits that will allow you to live the life you want. Clarity is a tool to purge those non-essentials, those distractions that are just causing you confusion and stress. Then you can get back to what is truly important.

How often do we get confusing information we must sort through? I had a very hard time when I was newly graduated from college. I was looking for work, and I also had some serious losses in my life, including my youngest brother and my ninety-six-year-old grandfather, who was very dear to my heart. As if that was not enough, I also had to end a long-term relationship.

This was way too much for me to take, and I felt that I was in a fog. Clarity seemed unreachable to me. One day I went to work and, upon seeing how decidedly not-okay I was, a coworker immediately took me to a bookstore and straight to the section where I could find a book on loss. I thought that either this person is extremely insightful, or I'm just walking around with a sign on my head that says *Help me, I am sad and I am lost.*

Either way, I was grateful to my coworker for taking

> *Clarity is a tool to purge those non-essentials, those distractions that are just causing you confusion and stress.*

the time to help me out when I did not realize that I needed it. I think many of us have to deal with our challenges silently; we have to be so strong because there is no room for weakness. We were not taught any other way.

I remember an occasion when my mother wanted me to come back home, while one of my friends who lived in another state was asking me to go spend time with them. At the time, I was working and I had my own place. I had just graduated from college, and I was not about to leave all of that to go mourn somewhere else. I had a whole life I had worked hard to create, and leaving did not appeal to me at all. I thought I could figure it out on my own.

I looked over the books in the loss section and found one entitled, *How to Survive the Loss of a Love* by Peter McWilliams and Harold H. Bloomfield.[23] It was a little book with paragraphs on the left page and poems on the right. What I appreciated is that I knew I could mourn for the losses in a systematic way.

Some people just forgo mourning the loss of something or someone that is very important to them, but the challenges that come from that choice, when you do not allow those feelings to come up and through you, show up just when you think they've been buried deep down. They will show up when you have another loss, and your reaction will be even more intense. Mourning is a very personal and practical need for humans. It is better to go into the sadness and pain in order to heal, so that you can honor yourself and what you have lost along the way.

How is clarity connected to meditating? When you

meditate, you can get rid of all that noise, and then you can see what you truly need. The book made me realize that the losses were extremely painful, sad, and uncomfortable and would likely continue to be for quite a while. However, I also had a friend reassure me that this too shall pass. In the book by McWilliams and Bloomfield, you are encouraged to set a time in your day to mourn, which means that you get on with your days as usual, follow your routines, but set special times aside to feel your feelings.

What I liked about this method is that I could feel the sadness engulf me for one hour in the evening every day. The authors also ask you to find projects or hobbies that you have been putting off and give them a try. I chose oil painting, so I bought a huge canvas, some brushes, and oil paints, and I started a one-year project; I worked on the painting steadily at least four times per week, and it brought me much joy. I also decided I wanted to sing, so I joined a choir at a church. One of my neighbors was kind enough to introduce me to the choir director, and I was able to sing with them, which was a sanctuary for me. I felt the love in those safe spaces that encouraged me to continue to heal from my losses.

I had not been meditating at this time, because I still thought that meditation was to stop migraines, and since I was not getting migraines, I was not meditating.

Even though I was steadily working through my loss, I was still in a fog, so I made an appointment with a doctor. He told me that physically I was fine, but I still felt that there was something wrong with my body. He asked me if I had anything else going on in my life. I told him I had recently experienced several losses in my family, to which he responded by giving me the name of a grief counselor. He said that my "dis-ease" was in my mind, brought on by sorrow, and I was baffled. Soon after, I made that call and I went to my first counseling appointment.

I was not aware that my mind could affect my body so much. When I read books and talked to the therapist I was seeing at the time, they said it was like having a broken leg no one could see. Healing from the loss would be like having a cast on your leg to allow the bone to mend. Mental or emotional sadness from losing someone is just like a physical injury; I find this to be fascinating: your mind is so powerful it can affect your whole body.

I did not feel well physically because of what was happening to me emotionally. I had to get my mind straight and deal with the losses, feel all the emotions. I had to experience the grieving and then the healing. I could not shove all of these feeling under the rug as I had been doing almost all my life.

There was no space while growing up to feel, but now that I knew about meditation and the help I needed through therapy, I could finally begin to heal.

During the year of grief counseling, my therapist and I talked about all the people that I lost. We talked about my feelings, and she gave me journaling assignments where I had to write letters to those I lost.

We also discussed my feelings with regard to my life in general after the losses. I talked about my life with those people in it, and then after they were gone. Some sessions were harder than others, but I kept at it and it helped a whole lot. Some sessions I would cry, and some sessions I would just be sad. It was part of the mourning and healing process. We also talked about what I was doing now and my activities outside of therapy. We would talk about anything and everything, and it was good to have that support during that time in my life.

After a year of therapy, my sessions with my therapist were more lively. I was finally happy again, and my therapist said we could stop. For the year that I was seeing her I was also singing in the choir, doing oil painting, and finally allowing myself time to mourn every night for an hour. I was actually doing a lot, but everything I was doing, although it was hard at first, actually ended up helping me with the grieving process. I allowed myself to truly feel my losses and be okay with them. I gave myself permission to know that this mourning process was a natural part of life, and although it was super hard, I was going to get through it. I felt so much stronger and more confident after I did all that work and allowed myself a proper year of grieving.

MOST HAPPY PEOPLE would attest to self-care; you cannot be happy and not take good care of yourself. Like I have mentioned before, your self-care and health are completely individual to you, and your methods are unique. The clearer you are on your methods and strategy, the quicker you will achieve happiness. And to achieve happiness, we must be true to ourselves. But why would we not be true to ourselves? Furthermore, why would we ever engage in self-deception? It makes no sense, but again, common sense is not so common.

Happy people are clear-minded people. Why would this be? The reason is because someone who has clarity finds it easier to get things done. People who have clarity know what the next step should be, and this in turn reduces anxiety and stress. There are many things that can make us unhappy; sometimes there is a lack of clarity, so we procrastinate because we are not sure what we should be doing next.

If we take the time to meditate in the morning, this can help us start our day in a relaxed manner and can help us have clarity throughout the day. We can have clarity by decluttering tasks that are not important for us to do, thereby getting rid of procrastination with clarity. And we can get this clarity simply by breathing in an intentional way that allows us to be present in what we are doing.

We think that we understand life as we live it, and that the way we experience life is the way it is for everyone. The idea is that you create your reality, and that is how you see the world. No one can tell you that you are wrong, not even you. But you have to ask yourself this: "Do I truly believe this is the way things are? Where is this idea or belief coming from, and do I believe it because I want to, or simply because it is all I know?"

Clarity is the idea that you can see something and understand it fully. For the most part, we all walk around in our insecure, underconfident way or secure, confident way, and all the while, we believe we are doing good. I think this attitude is great if you are clear on who you are and what you are doing.

But if you are not, then that is the journey to embark on. Some people think that others are wasting their time embarking on frivolous ideas that simply do not amount to anything. Say someone tells me a rumor that a person doesn't like me and I spend hours, days, weeks obsessing about it and turning it around in my head, only for it not to be true. Was I wasting my time thinking something to be true that was entirely untrue, something completely useless and unhelpful? These are the types of frivolous ideas we can get sidetracked by. Many of these things have to do with our perception of the world and what we think is happening. The main reason these are frivolous is because we truly cannot control anyone. Some people think they can, but at the end of the day, control is only an illusion.

We are constantly judged by our exterior, and that is just fine, but what about ourselves and what is happening in our interior? Most of us literally have to sit down and think about this. Yes, it is a lot of work, but the rewards are endless.

There are two things you get when you find this clarity. One is finding happiness. Knowing what is important to you helps you clarify your values. You have values and things in your life that are important to you, so you make time for them, and this makes you happy. Second, you do not waste time. If you are clear on what makes you happy, you can take action on your values now. This means you can be happy in the present. This is the opposite of putting off your happiness until you reach some milestone or get to some place, point, or destination.

This way you are happy during your journey as well. The final destination will not be the only opportunity for you to be happy; you deserve to be happy now, this instant. For example, if you get to your destination and you were not happy during the journey, you may think you have not actually made it to your destination. But maybe you weren't sure what happiness would've felt like, therefore, when you reached your destination, it was not what you thought it would be.

Knowing what is important to you helps you clarify your values.

MY MOTTO IN THIS LIFE IS: whatever works for you. Sometimes we distract ourselves and then we justify our distractions as being completely necessary, but it just causes you to focus on others instead of yourself.

I definitely was guilty of this; when I do not meditate and become clear on what is going on with me, I feel like I want to tell everyone else what is going on with them. Two things happen: First, I am not happy because no one really gives a thought to what you say, as it really is not your business what others are doing; and second, usually when we are unsure about ourselves, we want to be up in everybody else's business. We want to tell them how to live their lives because we're not really steady in ours. I tried this with my children, and they were not very interested in my goals for them. To be truthful, if we cannot even know what is going on with us and make ourselves happy, how the heck do we think we can help others? It doesn't make a lot of sense, does it?

We always notice the clearest person in the room. Do we want to immediately become friends with them? No! We usually feel uncomfortable with that person. We wonder, *How do they do it? Why are they so confident and secure in themselves? How did that person get to that place?* Then we start to think about how we could never be like that. *Oh, that person is just some sort of weirdo anyway; they may be delusional. Maybe they are on some sort of substance?* I have had people say that about me: How can you be so happy? Sometimes, I wonder if I was faking it until I made it, that I had put my façade back up again. My bouts of clarity were sporadic at best.

What I learned is that I do not have to prove myself to anyone; I do not even have to prove myself to myself. That is clarity—true clarity. That is what rest-and-digest is supposed to lead you to.

Clarity is power. Clarity is the peace that will take you from faking it until you make it to becoming crystal-clear about who you are, what you need, and ultimately, what makes you happy. This is all with no explanation, apology, or excuses to anyone, not even to yourself.

The reason that I have to say "even to yourself" is because when we talk about a higher brain and lower brain,

CLARITY

we need to remember that the lower brain wants everything to stay the same. It is not the one you have to convince, but eventually, you have to show your lower brain that your happiness is real, you mean business, and having clarity and health in your life is non-negotiable.

The ideas of a person being divided by different parts of their brains is not new. When we meditate, we can feel all regions of the brain become aligned; we are connected with ourselves. When we meditate, we give ourselves the time and space to become whole. This connection with ourselves creates clarity for our minds, and each time we meditate, it helps us move closer to it.

Of course, getting clarity comes easier to some than it does to others. When we are little kids, we are clear about who we are and what we want. Most children grow up as beautiful individuals. It is not until some adults or external world events start to shape the ideas of children that they doubt themselves.

For example, when I was young, I had a strong mother and she had lots of strong women friends all around her who were all entrepreneurs just like her. However, when I became an adult and started working, I learned that women were treated as weak, as if they were incapable of doing many things. This was an external world view that I did not share, so this was confusing to me, and I was shocked.

When children begin to get mixed messages that are not aligned with their internal sense of knowing, this is the beginning of their disconnect and confusion, neurological junk, mental clutter, and the list goes on. Basically, when children begin to think that they are not enough, they have mental stress and start feeling lost. The child then becomes an adult and in a sense loses their way. Did I lose my way when I became an adult and learned that strong women were not welcomed in a corporate environment? Yes and no: yes, because it did not make any sense to me, so I showed up in my power and was rewarded very well for it. No, because my collegues did not like that I did not fit the status quo and they tried to make me feel bad. Unfortunately for them, as a strong woman, I am not swayed by an external world that tells me to back down; I just shrug it off and say, "Hey, you do you, and I will do me." I did not care to weaken myself to make others happy, though I was pressured by my environment, time and time again. I always took a seat at the table with no apologies, and the funny thing is, I was always welcomed and admired for stepping up and participating. I feel happy that women are strong, though some women do not understand their own power, and that is also okay.

I show up for myself because when I was little I had to show up for myself; I had no choice. I feared getting lost in the fray, and I remember having tons of dreams where I was a lost child. I hated these dreams. I think it was my subconscious telling me to take my foot off the gas, to get myself off this roller coaster or treadmill and get back to the business of self-discovery. When we are children, we live in the present, and hence we live in discovery, but when this is turned off, we move into a place of stagnation and stress.

Since I was the second-youngest of sixteen kids. It was hard for my older siblings to always see me. So I had to try to get their attention; I had to show them that I could do what they could so they could invite me into their games. I always had to prove myself, which oftentimes seemed impossible because I was not tall or strong enough, but I still tried. Overall, I was a great success in corporate America because I grew up the way I did.

THE THOUGHTS OF NOT being big enough, strong enough, and tall enough to play games with my siblings could make me believe I was not enough. Although it may have been true as a child, if as an adult I hadn't thrown those old records away in my head or addressed them, they could have continued playing in the back of my mind. They would be the leak in the house, the energy drain that costs a fortune but gives nothing back. This is a useless way to think, a useless way to live your life and make your decisions.

We all have recurring feelings from different points in our lives. For example, remembering being left behind as a child because I had to take a nap and my family went to the dog racetrack without me leaves me feeling sad. I get sad because I remember that when I woke up and looked for everyone, no one was there, and then my grandparents told me they had all left for the racetrack. *Bummer*, I thought, *thanks a lot for thinking about me.*

Of course, as a child, we want to be with our siblings because they are our playmates, so when you get left behind, it is not a fun experience. But what story am I telling myself? If I play that record in my mind, then the memory of it becomes a habit. I can end up doing things that do not make me happy, or start making decisions to satisfy a need I think I have.

The key takeaway is if we do not know what we want because we do not give ourselves the time to meditate and breathe, we are basically reliving the past. We are a story, but we have the power to map it out and take ourselves where we want to go, to rewrite the story to fit our true selves. We have to write the story to fit what we need, what we love, and what brings us joy.

A story in my mind may go like this: when I was a small child, I had to keep up with all my older siblings. This was a lot of work. I knew that if I took a nap or relaxed, my siblings would go out and do something fun without me. Then, as an adult, this habit manifested in me driving myself to keep busy. I encourage myself to do things that make me feel like I am doing something productive. This way, I satisfy the story in my head that if I stay super busy with anything, no matter what it is, then I will not be left behind as I had been when I was a child.

While I was doing internal work on myself I realized two things: one, I am no longer that child that has to stay up with my older siblings; and two, in knowing that, I can let those negative feelings go. I can work on the things that bring me joy and not waste time on things that do not make sense for me today, in the present.

The clarity I have come to from doing meditation breathing on a regular basis is that I do not have to be busy all the time. As a child I constantly had to prove myself. I had to prove that I could stay up with my older siblings, that I was grown up and did not need to take naps. I laugh at this now as I imagine my five-year-old self valiantly trying to stay awake during nap time, pretending to be an adult. The memory becomes so sweet when I look at my younger self with my present loving eyes and see what a funny little kid I was. The past informs who I am, but its influence is not fixed.

ONE REASON FOR WRITING this meditation book was for me to create unconditional love for myself. I wanted clarity to meditate and to find out what I need to be happy, what I love, and how to accomplish this for my life.

Obviously, being one of the youngest in such a huge family could make someone confused and listless, so clarity was not a tool that was readily available for me to put in my toolbox. But what I have noticed as I become more transparent to myself is that I get to remove layers of things. These things are misconceptions, misalignments of myself and my inner being; these things are the confusion that unfortunately ran my life for most of my adulthood. The largest distinction I learned is that being successful and being clear are not the same thing.

Being clear is a job; it takes a lot of work. If there is

anything you take from my definition of clarity it should be this: clarity is true, unassuming self-love. It makes us real, so we can't fake it until we make it anymore. We do not need to be fake when we are clear on what we need to do to make ourselves happy. The reason you can be happy in finding clarity is because it feels like the chaos in your life lifts up and goes away from you, disappearing out of your eyesight and out of your life forever. If the world looks clearer to you, then you can see what you need and feel more confident in reaching for it. You will have a clearer picture of what makes you happy.

Now when you show up anywhere, like an event or occasion, you can show up complete and happy. You can show up as the real you, with no excuses to yourself or anyone else. You can show up happy, healthy, and successful.

We do not need to be fake when we are clear on what we need to do to make ourselves happy.

You no longer need to hide behind some façade. You are a person who listens to yourself; you are a person who knows themselves intrinsically, and the world celebrates you.

Meditation helps you become unassuming and just show up. The reason it helps you do that is because it gets your nervous system out of a knot. I like to use the nervous system as a reference point for two reasons: it connects both your mind and your body, but it also picks up on the energy in your environment, and both of these are important for your free movement in the world.

CLARITY

What is most interesting is that when you meditate, you can be at a frequency of true feeling. You are able to recognize the frequency that you are on. It may sound like a hokey idea, but studies have shown that whatever we think about and tell ourselves, whether we realize it or not, is what our brains register and pick up from our environment.

A widely known example of this phenomenon is our reaction to a statement like, "Do not imagine a purple elephant." Impossible, right? You will automatically gravitate to that image in your mind, though I told you not to. The mind cannot distinguish between "Yes, look at this" and "No, do not look at that." The mind just processes whatever you are giving it—kind of like a computer, and you are giving it instructions.

People want to numb out because they do not like the messages that are going on in their heads. I know that for a very long time I wanted to be numb, because I did not want to deal with all the thoughts that were on my mind: constant thoughts about my parents, my neighbors, my nephews, the topics discussed at the hair salon, and so on. When we are not clear on what our mind should be focusing or working on, it is a little tough for anyone to handle, and changing the channel is not an option, so we just try to numb it out.

Some people find this way of life boring, or they are skeptical of the happiness people are displaying with ease. I think the reason many of us decide to be "comfortably numb," as Pink Floyd sang, is because we do not know how to have quiet time with ourselves. We do not know how be okay with just being. The reason is we are constantly pulled in different directions, told to be this and also to be that. That is certainly one way to live, albeit not a very happy one. The other way to live is to feel: to feel marvelous in every single cell in your body. Yes, this is possible for everyone. You get to revel in the amazingness of who YOU really are.

Finally, you experience the homecoming you have always wanted—coming back to your happy self and your happy life that you always had within you. You finally get to go home to yourself. You get to invite other loving, caring, gentle, and amazing people into your house of happiness. You get to invite people to meet the real YOU, finally. You owe it to yourself to have complete clarity.

MEDITATION

YOU WILL REPEAT this exercise three times, and it takes about twenty minutes to complete:

1. Start by breathing thirty to forty gentle, regular breaths (your goal is to basically pay attention to your breaths and count them)
2. When you get to the final breath—breath thirty for example—you exhale for as long as you can, then you hold the breath out (twenty, thirty, or forty seconds is adequate)

3. Breathe in and hold your breath for ten to fifteen seconds
4. Repeat this three times, or as many times as necessary

This will clear your mind and relax you. Use this when you want to get clarity.

QUESTIONS

- Are your inner thoughts mostly positive? Mostly negative? How do you communicate with yourself?
- What is your definition of success? What is your definition of clarity?
- What destination are you hoping to reach? Are you finding happiness in your journey toward that destination?

07
WHY NOW?

"Growing pains are very real. And when children are struggling with an important new step forward, they sometimes have to push away their old habits rather violently. They don't need them anymore but partly they still do, so their behavior can be quite contrary and unsettling to those around them . . . The person may learn to do without satisfying the needs he feels he ought to have outgrown, but he is impoverished by the effort. We should grow not by turning against our earlier self but by building on its strengths. We should recognize that it served us well, but it's time for something else."
—Mildred Newman and Bernard Berkowitz,
How to Be Your Own Best Friend[24]

When I became a teenager my mom couldn't really give me advice like before because, in true teenage fashion, I thought she had no idea what she was talking about. It's the rite of passage for teenagers to start becoming independent by pushing anything and everything away from them and then immediately regretting some decisions. We get scared of all the power we now hold, learning how to deal with our big bodies and our newfound executive functions in our developing brains.

Well, my mom once told me that it would be better to travel through this world alone rather than with someone who does not have your best interest at heart. This advice confused me because at that point, most of my friends were actually my siblings, but I guess it made sense because I would be meeting many people who were not my family when I went off to college. Now that I could choose my friends, she wanted me to be sure that I chose wisely. Following her advice, I entered my friendships slowly to ensure that the people I was letting into my life had my best interest at heart. I was grateful that she gave me this nugget of advice, because I probably avoided a lot of betrayal and heartache because of it. Thank you, Mom.

You can read books on meditation, and you can start to meditate now, tomorrow, in a year from now, or you may decide never to meditate at all. The choice is yours. The choice has always been yours, and will always be yours; remember that.

Every day is a new day, and with every new day, there are more opportunities to be happy, healthy, and successful. You can be anything you want, even if someone tells you otherwise; you have all the answers within you. Meditating now will help you get to those answers sooner rather than later. Those answers that you get from meditating and breathing will help you start living the life you want now.

To be clear, this is not a linear process. Often I would start a meditation and breathing practice, and then inevitably I would put it down and get busy with something else. I finally got into meditating when I decided I deserved happiness every day of my life. I know that does not sound practical. Life is going to happen, good times and not so good times, but you have the power to focus on the good.

Now, walk with me here for a little while. What if I told you, you could have so many more good days than you have bad days; would you believe me? Maybe not, because you could say it's not realistic, that I have rose-colored glasses on. But we visualize what we tell ourselves to visualize. What if I tell you to look at purple elephants in your head; what happens then? You imagine purple elephants. Yup, there they are.

But what if I tell you to visualize a sunny day and feel the warm sun on your skin instead? Go ahead and close your eyes, and just imagine a beautiful sunny sky with the warm rays hitting your skin, warming you from the inside out. Did you feel that? You just did that with your mind. You just made that happen. I gave you the suggestion, you repeated it, and you made that nice feeling happen right now. You can make yourself feel positive things. Do you think you could make it a habit to feel this good all the time, or at least when you do your meditation? It's like taking that summer vacation without going anywhere; you get the same amazing feelings.

I wanted to be happy, and I decided that the time was now. Successful people are often happy because they block off ten minutes to an hour every morning to meditate and do breathing exercises. I thought, *Okay, do as successful people do, and you will be successful as well.*

I started to meditate and journal, and the next thing I knew I was writing a book about meditation. When I first became serious about meditating, it was just to be successful, but then my meditation also helped me deal with challenging times. I used meditation as a tool to create my life the way I wanted to live it: happy and with my eyes wide open, handling issues with grace.

Every single morning you wake up, you have a brand-new day, a brand-new breath, and you can create all your dreams. Yes, it does take a lot of work, and yes, every single cell in your body may say *Run away as fast as you can.* That's perfectly normal, but by meditating, you can learn how to start overriding that part of yourself that wants you to stay the same in order to not get hurt. It's part of the process.

This is a journey of self-discovery; it is a journey of self-care; it is a journey of unconditional self-love. It is the best darn journey you will ever take, and you can enjoy all your loved ones even more profoundly when you discover and recognize how amazing you are. Meditate to open the gate to your self-gentleness. Meditate now and open up a space for yourself. Meditate to find clarity, the beauty of having one hundred percent access to yourself: access to your heart, access to your true happiness, access to your sustainable and beautifully fulfilled life.

> *Meditate to open the gate to your self-gentleness*

Your body and mind want to protect you, so if there

WHY NOW?

are some big changes coming down the pipeline, your whole self may resist. This is perfectly fine and normal, as well as is the presence of both excitement and fear. The excitement is your higher brain, your higher self, the real you, ready for change. Your lower brain and body may be saying, *No, this is too weird; this is the stuff everyone warns us about; this does not happen in real life, and this does not happen to me.* But it does happen in real life, and it can and should happen for you, especially since you have taken the first steps to unconditional self-love by reading this book. You are saying "yes" to the Universe. You are saying, *I am ready to love myself. I am ready to give myself the space for self-discovery, for self-love, for self-care, for self-gentleness. I am ready to show up and show myself all these things. I deserve it*!

Perhaps you have heard the saying that the large rock was not broken by the final blow, but by all the blows before that. If we apply this to meditation, it works like a charm. Why? Because if you meditate for just five minutes a day, every day, you are the person hitting the large rock. All your little five-minute meditation sessions are never a waste. They will all be moving you closer and closer to your true bliss.

All amazing growth and change starts here. It only takes tiny shifts, small beliefs that you will at least try something. You are telling your mind, body, and soul that you mean what you are doing, that you are actively improving. When you meditate and do breathing exercises, you will start to see the difference in yourself immediately. Take my example of getting rid of migraines with meditation yoga: I really did not know what to expect, but that day changed my life immeasurably for the better. Who says it won't happen to you?

MY RELATIONSHIP WITH meditational yoga was rocky from the beginning. When I graduated from UC Berkeley, I tried to find yoga classes, but most of the places I attended did not do much of the focused breathing work. I still would do the meditational yoga if I felt that I was getting overstressed and to keep migraines away, but I did not get all the other benefits I could have gotten if I had been doing a regular practice of breathing and meditation.

Not doing meditational yoga and breathing exercises was actually a positive for me, because it led me to making meditation a habit, and therefore to writing this meditation book. It inspired me to write, not only so I can get you to meditate, but to regain clarity in myself, to remind myself why meditation is not about reaching milestones, but about creating lifelong habits, rituals, and routine practices that improve my life and allow me to be happy. Writing this means that I will not abandon it anymore, because for me, it would be like abandoning myself. My highest goal is to have unconditional self-love; this is what I strive for, and this is what writing this book has reminded me to reach for.

I became unhappy and unclear when I did not meditate, because the practice of meditation has always helped me relax; it helped me create positive energy, thoughts, or ideas and occupied my mind to keep me from uselessly worrying or feeling guilty about the past. I would get a bit angry and irritated that I had all these critical and worrisome thoughts. It weighed heavily on me, and then I would look out of myself and attack; I would blame this or that, this idea or that idea, this dogma or that dogma. I did not care who or what was my target, all I knew was that my mind, body, and soul were filled with useless information and ideas that I could not stop thinking about—ideas that made me angry, that scared me, that made me uncomfortable. I would get triggered and anxious for no reason. I did not know what was getting me so worked up, but I was feeding these negative thoughts; this is how I was operating in my daily life. I was a person in one big knot. The angry state of being I was in was probably my fight-or-flight response, keeping me so wound up that my only constant feeling was fatigue. Living this way just kept me in the fast zone, irritated and agitated, in the fray of anything and everything. When you meditate, it helps you get out of that fray. It helps you see other people and just love them for who they are. It helps you see that we are truly only trying to do our best. We are doing everything we can to live happy, healthy, and successful lives.

When I was tied in knots with all the useless thoughts hanging over my head, they were wasting my time. I always thought that others were the problem, but you cannot change others, no matter how hard you try. Trying to control others is a road that leads nowhere. Instead you are lonely, and you are just ignoring your real happiness and the things you really need. Go down another road; go down the road of meditation and find your home, your happiness, your self-gentleness, your self-care, and most importantly, your unconditional self-love. That road is so much more fun.

WHAT CAN YOU ACHIEVE with meditation? You uncover your higher self, your little voice, your universal connection, the real you. I know we think that the form we are in now is the real us. We often think: I am real. If I run in front of a bus, I will get hit and could get hurt. The real body and the real mind are there, but they can be two things at once.

Think about the real you as a person who absolutely loves you, takes amazing care of you, and is clear on all decisions. That self does not mind if you make mistakes; it is not judgmental, critical, or in any way hurtful to you. This is the real you. The real you is unconditional self-love; the real you is gentle, caring, and thoughtful to your needs. The real you takes excellent care of you. The real you never allows you to feel alone. The real you never allows you to feel as if you cannot handle whatever life gives you.

The real you never allows you to feel as if you cannot handle whatever life gives you.

The real you stands by you always and is a strong and powerful presence by your side; this is the real you. The real you helps you make decisions that allow you to continue to grow and be safe, happy, healthy, and successful. This is the real you.

For you to fake it till you make it, you must be someone else. When you meditate and you discover the real you, you do not have to fake anything; you can just show up with your unconditional self-love and do what you need to do. When we are operating from the fray, we tend to try to push ourselves to do things. Do not get me wrong; being the real you will not prevent you from doing things and advancing in your life. You will continue to dream big and achieve your dreams, but you will be doing it as yourself.

I know this can sound over the top, but let's look at people who are truly in their bodies, in their life, who are showing up. We want what they have. But often those things are achievable for them because they have meditation practices in their lives—nothing more, nothing less. When you give yourself time to meditate, you are giving yourself time to be the real you.

Should we compare ourselves to the outer world? If we do not, how do we know how we are doing, how we compare to others? Why would you want to compare yourself? Often it is because, either consciously or subconsciously, you think that you can find what you are looking for in someone else. But do those people know more about you than you do? Does your grandmother, great-uncle Marvin, or Tess down the road know more about you than you? That kind of thinking needs to change. Maybe when you were growing up the people around you tried their best, but they did not provide you with enough love or support. Maybe they were a nightmare and were screwed up, and in turn they screwed you up. Your truth and your life are yours to experience and interpret, and you are the one with the most knowledge on this particular subject. No one in this world can dispute your reality, because it is yours and yours alone. Sure, researchers everywhere want to find information and analyze it; these data mining companies and organizations want to be ten steps ahead of you and tell you who you are, what you need, and how you will react to such-and-such. On one hand, they are great at finding correlation and synthesizing large amounts of information, but take all their conclusions with a grain of salt because your unique set of circumstances may not line up.

The reason is that no data system will ever be smarter and more connected than a person. There is no way. That is why comparing yourself to the outer world, the external world, is futile and a big waste of time. The reason is that you are you and there can only be one you. I know that some people say if we are all special, no one is special. That thinking comes from people who do not practice gentleness with themselves; these are people who do not practice unconditional self-love. They are the people who are in the fray, and they may love it, they may live for it, it may make them happy, and more power to them. However, personally I have no interest in people who dismiss self-love, self-care, and self-gentleness as an excessive pastime. To have unconditional self-love is to be happy—plain and simple.

When I went to see the therapist after I had my skiing accident, one of the first things she said to me was to have self-compassion. I rolled my eyes and thought, *Not this again.* At that time, I thought that to be compassionate I had to live my life like Mother Teresa. Sorry guys, there is only one Mother Teresa, and she sure as hell is not me.

In hearing this stuff again, I was a little uneasy about my friend's advice to try therapy again. Since I had been working out twenty hours a week for my endurance run and now found myself bedridden due to my injury, and because I used sports as my way to numb out, they thought I had nowhere to go with all my feelings and my constant negative self-talk. It is interesting how sometimes our friends, family members, and people who love us guide us in the right direction. They guide us because they can see something that we cannot see ourselves, because we are not being self-aware.

> *To have unconditional self-love is to be happy—plain and simple.*

I was miserable during this time. I hated the idea that I could not move around. I was afraid to get knee surgery, and I was very upset and scared. I had been lucky enough in my sports career, up to that point, to have never gotten injured. I had completed nine marathons, done a bike ride of 111 miles, and could swim two miles at a stretch. I was completely happy with that, looking back, but at the time I was not satisfied.

Kristin Neff, a doctor of psychology from UC Berkeley, talks about self-compassion.[25] According to her, we can be too hard on ourselves, and we do not even realize that we are doing this. She says when your self-esteem leaves you, your self-compassion picks you up. She goes on to explain that comparing ourselves to others is futile, because it is not real. It only causes us problems, and even the people others compare themselves to are comparing themselves to others, so the bottom line is that it is a zero-sum game. Everyone is comparing themselves to everyone else in that type of environment, and it is both normal and sad. It cannot lead to happiness, but rather, it leads to you disconnecting from yourself; if your life is based on who you are not, then who are you? By doing this we are literally abandoning ourselves, and why would we do that? Sometimes it is easier to grab the low-hanging fruit than to do the work necessary to love ourselves unconditionally.

There is a reason for this figure of speech: do not compare your insides to other people's outsides. It is a simple concept that means that even though others may look fine on the outside, we do not know what is actually going on in their lives. Therefore, how can I compare my inside to someone else? I cannot know what they are feeling unless they share that information with me.

Regarding the self-compassion idea, I was incredibly skeptical about it and was not looking forward to doing all the work that my therapist was asking me to do in my condition. Look, it's not that I do not respect the work or the people that study this kind of thing, but at the time I was stubborn and clouded, feeling lost and afraid at the amount of work I would have to do on myself if I followed through on finding self-compassion. My lower brain was completely resistant to all this stuff, but because I was in a rather dire state, meaning that I could not use any of my normal numbing outlets, I had to deal with learning new skills, getting some new tools for my toolbox.

This meant change to my being, which meant that my body and all my cells would be resisting the changes, the knowledge. So I say again that we have the self that protects us, the lower brain, and then we have the self that takes care of us, loves us, and is gentle with us, which is the higher brain.

It is important to not compare yourself to anyone, because there is no one like you and there will never be anyone like you. You are unique. I work with lots of wonderful life coaches, and they all say variations of the same thing: "You must do you." You must live your truth. The more enlightened or happy the individual, the more they are in sync with who they are, and the more they understand who you are. The reason for this is that because they do all the necessary work to find themselves, they do not have to look at you to understand who they are.

If we are measuring ourselves through someone else's eyes, we are doing ourselves a disservice. First, if we cannot get our thoughts about ourselves clear, what makes us think we can do this for or about someone else? And the inverse is also true: Do we think that people who do not

If we are measuring ourselves through someone else's eyes, we are doing ourselves a disservice. know what is going on with themselves could possibly know what is going on with us? Even if they are experts in their fields and deal with this kind of stuff daily, it is almost impossible. Why do we think that someone out there could know more about us than we do? Many of us think this and live our lives this way. When we meditate we can turn off this idea and truly get to know ourselves. We can know what we need to make ourselves happy without looking through someone else's lens.

Even an advanced meditator must continue their practice of being mindful. Just like everyone else, they change and evolve over time, and their meditation practice can help them stay up to date with themselves and what makes them happy. To find out what we need, we meditate, take a break, and refuel our minds, bodies, and souls to stay clear and find the path. For us to focus on ourselves and find what we need is vital for our peace of mind. It is vital for our health. It is vital for our ultimate happiness.

We do not have to be the ones walking around clueless and possibly unhappy; we can be the ones who get to know ourselves better and find our own happiness. When we look outside of ourselves for happiness and we do not get to know who we truly are and what we need, we end up paying a price. Someone else cannot tell us how we feel or what we need; we are the only ones who can answer those very important questions. Our job then is to get to know ourselves. Yes, as I have mentioned before, it is a big job, but you were born to do it. You were born to be happy, healthy, and successful. You, and only you, can unlock the door to your happiness, and it is easier than you know.

WHEN YOU START to figure out who you are at your core, your life starts to glow and you get back to what you had when you first entered this world. At that time, you had lots of love, faith, and trust in yourself; you saw the world as a beautiful place. There is no way to know how meditation will make you feel until you start doing it, because it allows us to get off that neverending treadmill and find ourselves. By staying on and not giving ourselves a break, we feel tired and defeated, and we try—boy, do we try hard!—but we do not get that rest we seek. That is why meditation is so helpful, because it helps you get that relief; it helps you get back into your lane of love and clarity. It helps you get back to self-love and self-care, and it feels good. You are completely capable of doing this for yourself every single day through learning how to meditate. Then, when you show up for others, you show up from a place of knowing yourself, and this is such a beautiful place to be.

I was successful in my profession, home, and health, but I was still struggling to let go of my perfectionism so

> *Our job then is to get to know ourselves.*

I could fully be myself. This is what I saw when I met professionals in my career who were genuinely nice and also did great work. I liked that they seemed to truly listen. I felt that they were present when I talked to them, not mentally distracted by something else.

We all know who those people are: the ones who truly listen with their hearts. I always tried to be one of them, but though I tried to be respectful and available to others, I was not showing that respect and presence with myself.

Because I was not showing up for myself, I always felt like something was missing, that there was a part of myself that I was not acknowledging. The whole time, my happiness was fleeting or nonexistent. To the outside world it seemed as if I was fine, but in my internal world I did not quite know how to reach that happiness. When we think we are not showing up for others, we are really not showing up for ourselves. We are abandoning ourselves; we are leaving ourselves behind. I was not happy with this.

When we think we are not showing up for others, we are really not showing up for ourselves.

There are all sorts of self-help books out there; there are so many people who are truly happy, and they want to share that happiness with you. Something that always stuck with me were shows where the main character was trying to better their life, so they try reading self-help books as a strategy for self-realization.

The whole premise of these movies is that the person

reading the self-help book is not healthy or balanced, because they obviously can't do it on their own; they have to rely on the help of others. That internalized shame is why, when I would go on trips, I would take self-help books with me that weren't in English or whatever language was spoken in the place I was visiting. This way, no one would know that I was reading a self-help book, and then they could not judge me. In our society, somehow it is frowned upon for you to get healthy. Can you imagine?

At the present time in my life, I tell everyone about the self-help books I read. But a long time ago, when I was younger and did not have a lot of people around me who I could talk to about this stuff, I was doing research and getting better on my own.

The interesting thing is that even my children try to give me a hard time about the books I read. I am their mother, so you would think that they would have some understanding of how important and healthy this material is, but that shame is so strong and powerful. You have media and technology telling you, "No, do not read self-help books; do not love yourself; do not be so selfish; do not take good care of yourself in this way."

This book is not a tool to fight whatever messaging got to my children, and many children out there, that made them think that learning unconditional self-love is somehow not cool. I know now that I can only love my children, and they can do whatever they need to do for themselves. You see, part of the unconditional self-love journey is that you allow others to be themselves. The truth is, they

> *When you give yourself space, you give others space, and when you give yourself unconditional self-love, you give others unconditional love.*

all know what they need. Maybe today they need this, and tomorrow, they'll need that. The level of respect to allow people to be themselves is beyond the scope of this book, but I will tell you, this is necessary space. When you give yourself space, you give others space, and when you give yourself unconditional self-love, you give others unconditional love. Remember, you can only ever give others what you give yourself: no more, no less.

In having this space, we become less worried about what others think. As a matter of fact, we move away from the noise when we start to listen to ourselves and what we truly want. It is a journey of discovery, but why fake it till you make it when you could be on the journey coherently, enjoy the ride fully, and be able to get on with your life?

Let us think about today. As the saying goes: the past is gone, the future is a mystery, and the present is a gift. Most of us are happy receiving gifts, yet some of us have never felt the gift of the present. I mostly see it in people's eyes, the desire to let you know that *they are fine*. But behind their eyes, no one is showing up; they are both in front of us and far away. We miss the best parts of life when we are checked out.

Our mind does so well when we meditate. And it

doesn't just fix acute problems, like getting migraines from stress in college. Meditation helps with so much more. Meditation helps us learn about our minds. Meditation helps us learn that we can change our thinking.

Our mind is more than stress, more than being stuck and unhappy, but somehow we did not get the memo. So, I am giving you the memo now: our minds are so much more than the past or the future. These are all such simple concepts, but just because they are simple concepts does not mean they are simple to do. I wish they were.

I meditate every morning. Here I sit, writing this meditation book, and then my mind starts to wander. I know this is happening, because I like to go to my habit states, and those habit states are the ones that like to worry about the future or review any disappointments from the past. My job is to be present, because that is the only real thing there is, but my mind wants to jump around, because that is my mind's habit. Meditation helps you understand your world better; it helps you understand yourself better, and when you do this, you automatically live better.

Our minds are so much more than the past or the future.

When you are in the present, you are in flow, you are in discovery, you are in the now. Your brain is saying to you, *Thank you for taking such good care of me.* When your mind can have whatever you are doing now as its focus, it can relax, discover, and create. The frazzled brain that was trying to resolve the past or worry about the future is nowhere to be seen, and this is good for your health, your nervous system, and your life.

When you operate in the present for most of your time, you avoid burnout. When you meditate, you have more control of how you respond to your world, and therefore how you decide what happens next in your life. You walk in a state of clarity and get rid of confusion and oblivion. There is an element of control that we as humans have where we can control to a large extent how we can be safe, happy, healthy, and successful.

MEDITATION IS A PROCESS, and it is a lot of work. It is hard at times, but because it is so much fun, you do not realize how much work it is. The results of having a meditation practice are phenomenal, and you will wonder why you did not start sooner. It has taken me such a long time to implement meditation as a regular practice in my life. I try hard to do so because when I make something a regular practice, it becomes a habit.

I have seen so much improvement in my mind with things I have to get done, especially letting my family members off the hook when I want to micromanage them. I constantly want to help my children with their clothes, their homework, with anything and everything. My kids then tell me in no uncertain terms that they can do all this stuff themselves. I like that they are independent and do not allow others to control them; I can be proud of this fact. However, because they do not allow me to micromanage them anymore, I have to find a way to let these feelings out. I decided to meditate so I could deal with all that micromanagement energy I had as a parent.

I'm sure that you can think of a few things you'd like to improve on in your life. Now you must act, figure out when and how you will start to meditate. As I mentioned before, the easy way to do this is to just start and tweak as you go. I have given you a few very basic, beginner exercises to get you started, but since every journey is unique, chances are you may not be ready to stick to them for long, or maybe you are ready to make breathing and meditating a lifelong habit. The one thing I want you to know is that you must celebrate action, because the universe rewards it. Feeling better about yourself and your life by slowing down and breathing is a positive action, and you will reap the rewards.

As I write this, I think about what exactly that means. Dreams do come true when you start to meditate; happiness is a dream we all have, and we can all have this happiness now. There are lots of books out there on setting goals and finding out what your values are. I think that many authors would agree that part of the work is taking the time to listen to yourself—taking the time to slow down. Some of us do not give ourselves permission to do any of this for so many different reasons, but you are reading this book, so you are giving yourself permission, and this is good. The beauty of working on this is that it does not only help you, but all of humanity. It sounds like a lot of bull, but it's true. Healing yourself can and will heal others.

For example, if you walk into a store and the person helping you is hostile, or they are not even paying attention to you, or they are simply not engaged in their environment, you may not feel quite right. I can tell you that person most likely is not meditating, because if they were, they would not be so disconnected from themselves. That person is not doing a great job of plugging into themselves and their needs, and in this way, the interaction is lacking.

Healing yourself can and will heal others.

Now we have another example: you walk into the same store, but the person that is helping you now is very friendly. They greet you and are kind to you, and they pause and allow you to get your bearings by giving you space, time, and a gentle level of attention. You feel that this person is genuinely nice and completely present. You feel like this second person is well-rested and taking good care of themselves, because they appear to be coherent and helpful in an unassuming, confident, and friendly way, and you pick up on those vibes immediately. You carry a little of them with you.

Happiness, for whatever reason, is scoffed at. I know there are people out there that think if you are happy all the time, then there is something wrong with you. The truth is that these are decisions we make every day, and this does not mean that a happy person does not grieve.

It does not mean that a happy person does not care about others; it just means that some people know they reap more rewards if they focus on being happy.

If we grow up in a household where there is flexibility and unconditional love, we are given the space to be ourselves. When we are given this space it makes us happy, because we can stay connected with our true selves. When we grow up in a harsh environment where we are criticized and judged, we are taught to disconnect from ourselves, and this makes us unhappy.

When you show up for yourself, you are proud of yourself. You love yourself. You can appreciate others without having to control, manipulate, or using any of the other methods we try to hide our insecurities. People who meditate use it to manifest a better life for themselves.

So, you start the practice of meditating; you are bored by it, but you do it anyway, and you say to yourself, "So what if I am bored, I am still going to do it!" You eventually feel all the benefits and rewards that you get from meditating, and then you wonder why you were even hesitant to start a practice in the first place.

By simply showing up (as I did in the dimly lit gym at UC Berkeley), so too will you be healed and transformed from meditating. The thing is, when you do meditational breathing, you are telling your entire body, nervous system, and your brain: *I am serious, I mean business, and I am ready to be healthy, happy, and successful.*

THE POWER OF BREATH

SUCCESSFUL PEOPLE make decisions to do some boring stuff, but they do not call it boring; they call it healthy. They commit themselves to doing things that will clear their mind and make them be present. They do things that give them confidence. Simply by making the decision to meditate and acting on it, you have already started to set up the wiring in your brain for built-in breaks and therefore, you are already benefitting from just the idea of meditation.

Why is this important? It is important because we all need a break. The sad thing is that most of us are taught not to take breaks. People stress out, and we see it as a badge of honor. Do not get me wrong; hard work is a beautiful thing, and it brings great rewards with it. But burning out is not glamorous. When you meditate, you have no choice but to be honest. Not that you are being dishonest, but don't you want to find out if the person showing up every day is the real you, or just some version of you that you have picked up along the way, bits and pieces of who others have said you are?

Meditation allows you to make space for the real you. No one can give you that but you alone; some of us are so lost as to what we are doing and who we are that it is just easier to stay the same. But now there is a part of you that is saying, *Hey, I am here, and I am ready to show up. I am ready to be present and enjoy this amazing life.* Let yourself be happy, healthy, and successful by meditating, and watch the beautiful relationship with yourself manifest and grow.

Now does it make sense why so many successful people meditate? They do it because they honor themselves, and they show up, so in turn we see them and we honor them because they took the time to meditate, to do that hard work.

If you thought meditation was an easy job, think again; we are way too busy, and our brains and our environments are way too cluttered to achieve the level of Buddhist monks on the highest peaks of some sanctuary. We are normal people, but again, simply because we are not in the "ideal environment" does not mean that we cannot share in the life-changing benefits of meditation.

Meditation's largest benefit is that it will quiet your mind and allow you to let everything go. It will let you arrive at a place of peace in your heart, a place of peace in your soul. You will feel like you are being reintroduced to yourself. You will feel relaxed and wonder why you didn't start meditating sooner. Or, if you have not meditated in a long time, it will feel like coming home.

These are the things I know as a result of meditating regularly. It has changed my life for the better. I feel clearer and more in touch with what I need when I meditate. It helps me work through my life in a more coherent way. It helps me make better decisions for myself and say what I mean and mean what I say, which gets me more of what I truly want, rather than what I think others want for me. It also helps me relate better to my husband and my children in a more kind and compassionate way. I can truly listen to them and respect them. I can also ask for what I want and I get the same level of respect from them. Overall, it has helped us grow as a family by allowing us to show up as who we are without pretense, and it has also allowed us to unconditionally love each other even more.

The largest and most life-changing aspect of meditation is to actually live a real life. This means not hiding behind anything, a habit that does not work to our advantage and actually hurts us. When we do not know what is truly inside us, we will look outside for solutions, knowing full well the answers we're looking for aren't out there. We know that intuitively, but we do not really stop to think about it. Worse yet, we do not give ourselves time or space to view what we truly need.

MEDITATION

THIS MEDITATION IS self-care breathing to get you through low-energy times of your day.

Take twenty gentle breaths while having both hands on your heart in order to ground yourself.

Here we will allow ourselves to show up.

Start by thinking about the time of day that is usually the most challenging for you. Once you have decided, set up some guard rails; you want to pay special attention to self-care during those times.

For example, let's say you decide you need some energy in the evening; you can do your breathing exercises, have some chamomile tea, listen to relaxing sounds such as a piano playlist, or even allow yourself a moment of simply sitting quietly.

Your main goal is to be there for yourself and take the opportunity to take extra good care of yourself by not allowing yourself to get stuck in toxic, negative thinking that is normal when energy reserves are low. Go into your body through your breath and gently think of each part of your body: your feet may be tired, your shoulders may be stiff, whatever it is. Go into these parts of your body and send relaxing thoughts to them and enjoy your breathing, chamomile tea, or your relaxing music.

Say no to anything that is not nourishing your mind, soul, or life and move on to taking care of yourself, knowing that you will have your energy reserves back very soon. Self-awareness is key to knowing when you will need self-love the most.

QUESTIONS

- Do you ever find yourself comparing your insides to other people's outsides?
- What are some tangible ways you are trying to improve yourself?
- Do you feel you are the real you, right now?

08

HEALTH

"A few years ago, when my son was about three, I tried something new. I had come downstairs at 5:30 a.m. and meditated for ten minutes. Sometimes I felt, 'What was the point of that?' All I was doing was going through my to-do list for the upcoming day in my head. But on other days, I hit the zone a little more. Slowly, I found my energy levels getting better. I was not as reactive—I was not responding to things in the instant. I did not get so cross in the car. My sleep improved. I was able to focus more on my work. Even though during some sessions, I could not switch my mind off at all and was sure the meditation had been a complete waste of time, it did not seem to matter. The effect remained."
—Dr. Rangan Chatterjee, *How To Make Disease Disappear*[26]

My grandmother's death was very traumatizing for me. I loved my grandmother so much that when I was small, I used to think, *When Grandma dies, I want to die with her.* This was the same grandmother who used to take me to the movies, who gave me all her beautiful empty perfume bottles so I could play with them: The one who bought me my very first tea set, which I absolutely loved and played with on a regular basis. Grandma allowed me to help her in the kitchen while we prepared food for the week; I was mostly just playing, but she made me feel so special and helpful. I loved my grandmother; I was able to be a real kid when I was with her. For example, I used to pretend that I had a perfume shop and that my customers would come into my little shop. I remember having tons and tons of tea parties. I remember my grandmother braiding my hair for kindergarten. I have so many wonderful memories with her.

Sometimes we do not have time to think about our health, or worse yet, we do not want to talk about it. We feel better just avoiding the subject of our health all together. This counterintuitive view of our health makes sense to us, because many of us do not know where to begin with taking a real look at ourselves and how we can be happier and healthier.

As Dr. Chatterjee states in the quote above, he felt some days that the meditation he was doing was useless. This is a doctor who is feeling like what he is doing isn't making a difference, yet in his everyday life, these little habits of breathing and taking time to meditate are making key differences. He said his energy levels were better. He said he was more calm in the car. This is similar to what you and I go through on a daily basis. We all have to get things done, and if we put more stress or less stress on ourselves, the difference will determine if we are healthier or not.

HEALTH

When trying to start a new habit, often I would not see immediate results, so I wanted to throw in the towel. My mind would call it a waste of time, but my experience and my wisdom would say that it mattered. I tell myself that it will make a difference, so I should do whatever I needed to do to reach my goals. When I say this, it is easier to get what I want to get done.

I feel that there is a gap when we are building new habits. For example, when I was in high school, I would wake up every morning at four o'clock to get all of my homework done. This was a habit that I built over time. I was able to maintain this habit because I liked education and I wanted to ensure that I would go to college. I also remember using the same study habits I practiced in high school when I started community college to get my associate's degree, and these habits were so strong after doing them over and over that I was able to not only apply but also to get accepted to UC Berkeley. I liked the fact that if I built the habit and put in the time and energy, I would get the results I wanted. It helped me be patient and also enjoy the results when I reached my goals.

When I do not meditate, my health seems to diminish. It is subtle, but I do not do all the things I want to do. I tend to want more outside sources for my energy: more coffee, sweets, and junk food. I actually do not like any of that stuff and always both physically and mentally feel better when I eat wholesome food, but when my energy stores are depleted and I do not know how to get them back up, I just reach for those havoc-wreaking foods.

It just makes me more upset, because my body does not want it. My internal self is saying, *Hey wait, I not only do not like all that stuff, but it makes me feel sick.* So, the quick fixes are really neither quick nor fixes, and I can't even enjoy them. When we look at this from a health perspective, if I am meditating and breathing (mostly focusing on what is happening with my breath) then I am getting a real view as to what my energy stores are and what I can and cannot accomplish by the end of the day. The breath acts like a system that tells you how much energy you have in your tank. For example, electric cars will give their owners a reading of how many more miles they have left before they have to charge the battery. So if you are breathing within a rest-and-digest framework, then you may have quite a bit left in your engine and can continue to work on your projects for the day.

However, if your breathing is shallow, or if you do not want to even think about your breath because it is a waste of time and this meditation junk is useless, then that is a red flag indicating that you need to slow down and start to monitor your breath. This does not mean monitor your breath as if you are not breathing, because obviously if you are reading this you are breathing, but what I mean is that you monitor your breath by getting in touch with it.

If you are paying attention to your breath, then you do not have to reach for the unhealthy habits you are accustomed to. The reason is, if you monitor your breath you will be taking care of yourself and your immediate needs. You might not have to get a smoke, junk food, a

HEALTH

drink, or whatever your choice is for overriding your real need to take care of yourself, and hence you improve your overall health.

Yes, breathing work—just noticing and learning about your breath—is this powerful, and it is free. If you took this to heart and built a whole system of habits around breathing and paying attention to your breath for six months, you would go to your doctor and they would be surprised by your health levels. My world has been transformed by simply paying attention to my breathing, and yours can be, too.

When I am not paying attention to my breath, I am relying on external sources to get my energy. I feel out of sorts and I am not being clear or honest with myself. For example, if I am reaching for junk food instead of meditating and focusing on my breathing, I can literally see the negative impact those choices make in the long run. Then I go get my blood analyzed by my doctor and they tell me, "Hey, lay off the sugar, or you are going to get diabetes," or "drink less coffee or you will get high blood pressure and you will not be able to sleep at night," or "junk food makes your cholesterol go through the roof, and you might get a heart attack."

For me personally, these are all the result of not meditating and doing my breath work. It sounds so simple. So, why then was it so hard for me to do my breathing exercises and meditating for my health? This is such a good question, but there is no one answer. Simply paying attention to my breathing gives me a healthier way to live. Yes,

THE POWER OF BREATH

it is that simple, especially when you work on it to make it a part of your everyday life.

Before I decided to do breathing work again I would respond to my doctor in the following ways: "I get what you are saying doctor, but I get so stressed out that I cannot relax and my sleep suffers, or I cannot get enough energy because I have a million things to do, so I reach for the sugar to get a quick energy fix." Then the doctor says that although we are all tired and overworked, these types of habits are going to kill me, and that I need to find a better way.

But what can I do if I am just a victim of my circumstances, a victim of this fast-food nation I live in? This stuff is so addictive, you'd have to be a superhero to resist. But am I a victim who cannot save myself? To be clear, no food, coffee, or junk food is off-limits; that is definitely not the point I am trying to make here. What I truly want to say is that these things are just what they are, they are options for all of us—just not the best options.

Many of us live a life full of responsibility. Many of us have long commutes, long bus rides, car rides, and plane rides. We have to get up early in the morning and we go to sleep late at night. We live with people who have their own needs. We have big responsibilities, and the work appears bottomless. Some go to church and pray, and this helps them get relief and recharge, while others do yoga for the same purpose. Some socialize with people they love and care about, and this helps them get relief and recharge.

I know I need to meditate in order to rest and digest.

HEALTH

I need to meditate and do easy breath work so I do not rely on coffee, sugar, and junk food. To reiterate, I am not saying there are foods you shouldn't eat. No, that is not my point or my place to tell anyone any of this. What I am asking is: What are you paying attention to? Are you thinking about how you are refueling yourself, and are these ways healthy and sustainable enough for the long haul? Are you listening to yourself? Are you listening to your breathing? You simply have to give yourself a chance to truly listen to yourself. Our challenges start with us and how we are moving around in this world.

Your breath will give you a crystal-clear view of how you are truly doing and what it is you truly need to make yourself healthy, happy, successful, and satisfied.

Life is a journey, and meditation, along with other healthy practices, will get you to where you want to go. It is an easy and literally cost-free way to start getting you reconnected with yourself. My health has definitely improved with meditation. When I think of the times I have been my happiest and healthiest self, it is when I am meditating. And since I have picked up my meditation practice as a habit, I no longer crave sugar as something I need to have in order to get by.

Our challenges start with us and how we are moving around in this world.

I now have a routine suggested to me by a life coach in which I meditate every morning for twenty minutes. It helps me relax and clear my mind early in the morning.

I like it because it helps me gently get out of bed, fully refreshed and happy.

Your life-changing benefits may look completely different than mine, but what I do want to tell you is there is great happiness and joy in figuring out who you truly are and what you love. This is for real: not what you think your mom, your spouse, your boss, your neighbor, your pets, or strangers on the street want for you. You are the number-one person in your life, as you should be, because you are meditating and taking the time to listen to yourself.

Some health benefits of meditation are reduced stress, better sleep, and even better levels of blood pressure. For me, not only is the health of the body important, but the health of your mind as well. Your executive brain needs those health benefits to make decisions. This affects your health by simply allowing you to create habits that truly benefit you. The bottom line is that deep down, we always know what is going on with us; we always know what we need.

We are constantly bombarded with diseases, ailments, and tragedies. It happens, and it's a hard fact of life that we all have to face. But also remember the other side of the coin: that we can have compassion for it, but we do not have to internalize it so much that we get ourselves sick as well.

I am not certain why we tend to do this as humans. We tend to get sick when someone else is sick. Sometimes I wonder if it is because we have way too much empathy.

HEALTH

We also have to think of our health as an important element in our happiness. If we do not have our health, this makes our lives more difficult. To feel grief without relief is to sweep it under the rug, and all that does is affect our health down the road.

There is a difference between having compassion and being empathetic to the point of getting sick ourselves. I will not debate this point, as it is hard for me to walk in everyone else's shoes, but what I have learned is that it is one thing to deal with the realities of grief in a healthy way and another thing to deal with the realities of grief in a harmful way.

When you meditate, you can deal with the tragedies of life and also bounce back sooner. The reason for this is that you do not stay indefinitely in a state of sadness, but you can move within your grief, which is important, and also get on with your life. When you meditate, you give yourself a break from the external world, and this way, you have a bit more control over how you want to deal with different events in your life. When you do this, it will help your overall health.

Think about a time when something very hurtful happened to you. You probably felt very bad, mad, or even numb. People deal with tragedies in many different ways, and your body probably felt certain feelings in order to cope. Let's say that your body automatically shut down, or you got a pain in the pit of your stomach and felt like you wanted to throw up, or you felt a surge of anger. Whatever it was, you were affected by the reality before you.

The reaction your mind and body had was the right reaction for you, and the reason you got a reaction is because the pain was hard to bear, so your body did whatever it could to protect itself. When something tragic or sad happens we want to get away or pretend it did not happen in order to cope.

If we look at this through an emotional lens, it makes sense. For example, when I had all my losses, three of them at the same time, and I did not feel well, I had to make an appointment with the doctor to help me figure out what was wrong with me. The doctor told me the losses were affecting my health: no broken leg, just a broken heart. No one can see it, but the doctor knew that I needed to see a therapist to grieve, mourn, and most importantly, heal from all the loss.

I also learned that I could walk around sad yet functional, and then I could also do my work and still schedule time to begin the mourning process. My understanding of the mourning process is that it's a healing process. For example, if you break your leg, you have to let it rest and get stronger. You go to the doctor to let them know you broke your leg, or you think you did. The doctor takes some x-rays, then sends you through an MRI machine. The doctor puts on a cast, lets you know about how long it will take for the bone to heal, and advises you to stay off your leg in order to allow the mending of your broken bone to take place. When you have a loss, none of this happens, but it really should. Some people think that there is no time for this; there is nothing that physically shows them there is something wrong with them.

If I scheduled an hour in the evening, I could give myself space to cry and to feel all the emotions of losing someone. I would be flooded with the feelings of the loss for an hour; I was usually alone in my bedroom, as this is where I felt was my safe space to do this type of healing work.

Once the hour was done, I put myself back together emotionally. I was always extremely exhausted by all the crying, releasing the pain that comes with losing people you love. The funny thing was that I actually felt good when I was done, like I could have a restful night's sleep.

The health benefits of mourning are so vast. Most of us do not want to feel the pain of sadness or loss. This makes sense, as the feelings are strong, and they are not truly allowed in many cultures. If you cannot live your life because you are consumed by all the loss, then you can actually die if you stay in this state. Many of us do not know how to do it in a healthy way, or we think it is wimpy and stupid; if you cry then you are weak. But if you can schedule some time to cry at night, then you can live your life as best as you can, while not forgetting that healing needs to take place.

Thankfully, I was able to go full swing into the healing process and was happy that I could set out some time in my busy schedule to dive into mourning. What I truly loved about this was that I could accomplish healing and not pretend that the losses did not happen.

Then the next day, I would go to work and do my day

activities, and then again at night I would set my hour of mourning to cry and grieve and allow all those sad feelings to come out. At first it seemed a bit weird, but the more I did it the more I got used to it, and the more I started to feel better. It was such a cleansing time for me.

When I started giving myself that hour every night to grieve, it was extremely hard. I felt like I had no clue how I was going to be able to do this every night, but I soon learned that it got easier. I was able to truly be there with the loved ones I had lost, was able to let them go and be okay with the truth of what was going on in my life. I would wake up the next day refreshed and happy that I was not avoiding the sadness and pain from losing those I loved, but that I was actually doing something about my situation.

For those of you who need to grieve and have never had the space to do it but realize that your body wants to heal, you must definitely find the time to grieve and heal yourself. You should do this, because you want to feel your sadness and you also want to feel the sadness of others.

You can actually schedule time to heal old wounds, say for ten minutes, and then you're done with it. You do this as many days as you need, as many times as you need. What is important to understand is that if you do this, you know you are honoring yourself and your pain, and you don't have to walk around with this sadness all day, because you have now scheduled time to heal from it.

Each of us, if we take a look inwards, will find what makes us happy. If we look outside of ourselves to tell us what we need to be happy, we may find things that bring us some happiness, but we eventually find that it was fleeting at best.

I know that many of us like to base all of our ideas and decisions on science, and who doesn't want to do this? However, these conversations with ourselves cannot be easily quantified or examined, so science doesn't help us heal in that regard. It does not mean that I am so "zen" that I could walk in front of a bus and believe nothing would happen to me. No, that is not what I am saying. I understand that there are some truisms out there, some universal laws, like gravity or Newton's laws. What I am saying is that there is so much more that you can learn about yourself beyond the scope of what you can see and hear, and meditation will help you do this.

HEALTH IS AN EXTREMELY sticky subject, and the reason I say this is because some of the information on health can be highly personalized. Advice that is beneficial for one group may not be for another. The bottom line is that you need to find out what works for you. Remember, when you are meditating, you are tapping into your true self and your true needs, not your friend's, not your neighbor's, not your grandmother's, not the head of your organization. You get the picture.

We like to work in packs; we like to belong to something bigger, as we are social creatures, and that is okay and very healthy, but for you to find out what you need individually is also healthy. It is imperative that you know who you are and what you need, because this is how you shed the fake-it-till-you-make-it persona that is meant to fake everyone out—even yourself.

Your health depends on you being true and authentic with yourself and putting in the work to take good care of yourself, to honor yourself, and to stick up for yourself. What that means is that your health is only in your hands and no one else's. When you meditate, you can find out what it is you need for your health. Do you need a break, sleep, to participate in a sport or hobby, to work on your proposal immediately when you get home for one hour after dinner with your family? These are part of your health; these decisions are part of you functioning in this world at your highest level. These are the questions and solutions that will keep you free from heart attacks, from strokes, from being on medication for the rest of your life.

You may be thinking: *No way can one little addition to my life do that for me. This is all a lot of BS.* Isn't it a crazy idea that something so simple and accessible as meditation could turn your whole life upside down, that you could do it anywhere and see the benefits immediately? Well, it is the truth, and I am happy to be giving you this information.

Let's examine how this little lotus plant, or this little acorn, can transform your life. There is an amazing author, James Clear, who wrote the book *Atomic Habits*; I am a sucker for this author, and I will tell you why.[27]

Intuitively, I have been practicing what he writes

about for all of my life, and I just did not know what it was called. Also, as you will learn, once you start getting into meditation as a daily practice, you will start seeing, hearing, and feeling the same sage messages that have been handed down from generation to generation, everywhere.

The whole idea behind James Clear's book is that you start with small habits, do those consistently, and you can start to see the results over time. Now that is a lot of improvement, and meditating will help you make those tiny improvements that will surely collect and multiply. If you have a chance to read the book, you definitely should. I recommend this book to many people as a great tool for those of us who feel we are way too busy for something new.

When we think of health, we must remember that to be happy is healthy and to be honest with yourself, even if it is hard work, is healthy. To show up for yourself and be present in all that you do is healthy. To have people who love you, care about you, and respect you is to be healthy. These are all healthy things, and every one of us is entitled to have such basic human benefits in our lives.

The point is that if you meditate, you benefit; your health will benefit because you give yourself breaks. You give yourself a break from comparing yourself to this person or that person, this thing or that thing, or whatever it is that makes you think that you need something outside of yourself to make you happy. Meditation reminds you that all along you hold everything within yourself. And this is what meditation offers you: a chance to learn who you are and what you need to be happy, healthy, and successful.

I know this seems like the biggest lie ever told by anyone, but it is true. We are not Mother Teresa, bless her soul; we are just regular people who are trying to figure out our lives. We are just trying to survive and thrive. It is all possible with meditation. Our health, our livelihoods, depend on us acting for ourselves.

Meditation is important to our health simply because we mess ourselves up when we try to find solutions "out there" and not within. I obviously do not have all the answers; my journey, my path, and my life have not always been ponies and rainbows. There have been many thunderstorms, losses, and illnesses, but my meditation practice helps me weather the storms of life. I know we all want that, and we want to be able to stand tall when the storm passes; we will clean the mess up, the whole time knowing we are okay, and we will continue to be okay, even with the storms.

> *Our health, our livelihoods, depend on us acting for ourselves.*

We can explore, discover, and enjoy this world while we are alive. The idea is that we can tell the story in whichever manner we choose. The vocabulary we use influences our thoughts and our lives. For example, if in the story we are telling ourselves about the world is limited to a couple of good words and tons of bad, sad, and depressing words, to what extent are we making ourselves unhappy?

A benefit of meditating for your health is that you have that time to process feelings; you do not shy away from them, you do not bury them deep inside of you and pretend they are not happening. You deal with them, you face them, and you know you will always be okay.

I know this sounds like a tall order, and to be clear, it is a tall order, but you are not reading this book to get nothing for your investment. You deserve to go on this journey with happiness in your heart—authentic happiness, not the fake-it-till-you-make-it kind. You are a real, genuine person, so you do not have to fake anything; if anyone must fake it, it is the people who do not want to meditate and find out who they really are. Let us show up and enjoy each other's beauty and company.

MEDITATION

Here are several breathing meditations you can utilize, depending on how much time you have.

If you do not have a lot of time, do this:

> *Breathe in for three seconds, hold for four seconds, breathe out for five seconds, hold for two seconds (Repeat five times)*

If you have a little more time and you want to have a proper relaxation, do this:

THE POWER OF BREATH

Breathe in for four seconds, hold for five seconds, breathe out for six seconds, hold for two seconds
(Repeat ten times)

If you have a lot of time and you want to take your breathing to the next level, do this:

Breathe in for five seconds, hold for seven seconds, and breathe out for nine seconds, hold for two seconds
(Repeat ten times)

If you have been doing breathing exercises for a while, do this:

Breathe in for seven seconds, hold for nine seconds, and breathe out for eleven seconds, hold for two seconds
(Repeat ten times)

This exercise is for getting stronger lungs, not necessarily for relaxation, but it helps you with easier meditation breathing when out in public:

Breathe in for nine seconds, hold for eleven seconds, and breathe out for fifteen seconds, hold for two seconds
(Repeat ten times)

HEALTH

QUESTIONS

- How have you dealt with grief or loss in your life? Did you give yourself enough time to process your feelings in a healthy way?
- Have you seen how a negative mental state has impacted your health or that of those around you?
- What is your inner monologue like?

09

HAPPINESS

"Be in a good mood—for no reason. We feel better, in general, when we are in good moods. For whatever reason, that is true. We take on more challenges and live with more gusto when our mood is high. However, you do not need to wait for a reason to be in a good mood, as many people do. While a call from a friend, praise from your boss, or thoughts of upcoming weekend plans can certainly boost your overall feeling of well-being, how about bringing that same feeling into your daily life for no specific reason? It is something you have the power to do, and you will reap the benefits."

—Mary Jones, *Believe in Yourself!*[28]

"I will be responsible for my own happiness. Every day, I will do something that feeds my soul."

—Amara, HeatherAsh, *The Warrior Heart Practice*[29]

When I was very young I was naturally curious, and I was in a good mood most of the time. My mom taught me to appreciate a sunset, a beautiful flower, the smell of freshly fallen rain. She was always pulling the beauty out of life and I loved this about her. I remember she would tell me to look at a certain painting, a particular building, or the vibrant color of an outfit. She also regularly loved to make beautiful things: a floral arrangement, clothes, to have the house decorated nicely. She also took pride in always being dressed and ready to go out to the grocery store if she needed something for dinner. She loved to get up early and be ready for her day. Now that I think about it, this must have been such a good habit for her, as I am sure sometimes she was exhausted. However, positive habits can help make you happy just to be happy. Now that I am an adult, I still love to look at the beauty of life. I can get lost in the leaves of a tree, the flowers that grow among the trails that I walk on. I go to museums and enjoy the wonderful artwork. This all makes me happy. Thank you, Mom.

IN MARCIA WIEDER'S book *Dream*, she talks about how to live a life with purpose.[30] One of the essential ways to do this is to create a meditation practice for yourself so that you can stay clear on what you are here to do in this world. Wieder is a big advocate for every person looking into their hearts and finding their superpower. She wants people to find the thing or situation that hurt them and see the reality: that it is something that happened, but the growth and learning that came from it are a gift. I recommend reading her poignant book for more details and examples.

You deserve happiness, you deserve to live an amazing life, and you deserve to be spectacularly you and share your gift with the world.

Do not feel too much pressure to completely change and transform your life right away. You can simply start with baby steps and begin by using breathing and meditation to start learning how to relax and de-stress. You do not have to increase the expectations of yourself. Who has time for that?

The key is to stick to the breathing exercises as a life long journey. Though you will find the meditation very helpful immediately, sticking to the practice for a long time is what actually changes your life, what is transformational and life-changing. Yes, this means that your clarity from meditation will take you to so many amazing places you may not be aware of yet. You will experience the real deal of happiness, the kind that you feel in your heart and every cell in your body, the kind that shows you that you are loved and cared for. When you give yourself this space to meditate and reconnect with yourself, the dreams you have been keeping safe deep down inside will eventually show up. I know, it is exciting stuff!

How often do we stop a routine that we have picked up, once it has helped us? We think, *Okay, great, I feel better now, and I can move on*. I know when I have used meditation in the past, it was this way for me. Therefore, I am writing this book as a commitment to myself to continue my practice indefinitely: my commitment to myself that I am willing to do the things necessary for me to succeed in my pursuit of happiness. I realize some challenges and setbacks are inevitable and normal, and I am actually okay with that. The meditation and breathing allows me to experience them without becoming derailed. This allows me to keep to my commitment to being happy and enjoying my life, no matter where I am.

The benefits of picking up any meditation practice are so powerful that we should do it simply because we can. What I would like you to take from this is a practice of meditation on your terms, where you do not have to explain anything to anyone. You do not need permission to pick up something that is life-changing, something that is simple, free to do, and ultimately a net positive. I aim to continue to move toward my goals of living an amazing, fabulous life and gain success, health, happiness, and satisfaction. This is happiness. Remember, simply because you can be satisfied with your life and all the wonderful things you do does not mean that you cannot continue to think big or go for more goals. The journey is simply one of discovery, curiosity, and of course, happiness.

How many of us blame what happens to us on something outside of ourselves or play the victim game? Even some apparently healthy people do this; if they are blaming others for their problems, they are still trying to find something outside of themselves to help them feel better. Spoiler alert: it never works. Therefore, I have also made the commitment to take full responsibility for my success. I am committed to taking personal responsibility for my life and my success, however it looks to me. I promise myself I will commit to taking personal responsibility. This allows me to be in the driver's seat of my life, and yes, sometimes it can seem a bit scary, because if I screw up it is all on me. But then again, the opposite is also true; if my life is awesome and amazing, it is all me. You are the driver in your own life, and your choices are the outcome of how you choose to live it. It's as simple as breathing: breathe in happiness, breathe out happiness. You got it! It is both scary and liberating at the same time.

Think about it this way: you meditate, you breathe, and you start to toy around with this future vision of yourself. It feels completely awkward and phoney, and maybe you are thinking, *This is the fake-it-till-you-make-it, which you have been telling us not to do.* Yes, and no. Yes, because it will feel uncomfortable for you to visualize yourself in the life that you want, but no, because the difference is that you are okay with feeling the weird signals your lower brain sends all through your body. You are not pretending you are not feeling the feelings; what you are doing is being okay with the feelings, but you are starting to create a brand-new neuron in your brain for what you truly want and allowing yourself the discomfort of trying on your happiness.

We can't always blame others for our own shortcomings, but the stories we tell ourselves are very powerful. We know we can take full responsibility for our lives and our happiness. We know better, but we do not want to do better because it is scary, it is the unknown; what if we meet our real selves and we are so utterly disappointed? What if we take the time to do some serious self-awareness work and we find it is too hard to handle? We have some harsh realities to face. We are just getting by and not truly connecting with ourselves day in and day out. This may be your story or it may not be. If it is, let me tell you, it is awesome on the other side, where you get to know yourself and find out how truly awesome you are.

It is work, and it is worth it. You are worth it, and don't let anyone ever in this life tell you that you are not worth it, because I am here to tell you you are worth it, and you know deep down in your heart that you are. Breathe into your awesomeness, breathe into getting to know yourself fully, accepting yourself fully, and having unconditional love for yourself fully. It is about time for you to be totally happy, healthy, successful, and satisfied.

This is powerful stuff, and it is difficult; it is painful that we are so off-track with our true selves sometimes. I laugh at myself, and I laugh at you, and I laugh at us, because we are all essentially just lost children, trying to find home.

Why not be happy and flexible as we lose ourselves?

At some point, we are all trying to figure life out, every day. So why not be happy and flexible as we lose ourselves? Why not be enlightened about what type of connection we want for ourselves? Why not show up for our own selves and connect with ourselves?

As I write this, I have an internal feeling that this is all nonsense. But then my higher brain tells me that this is what it's like to be human, to be alive, to show up for yourself. I know that I always want to have it all figured out. This is what the cells in my body, what my lower self requires, but my higher brain knows that each day is a chance to connect with myself and the world. I think that my lower brain has had to function in fight or flight all my life and it is just exhausted. It doesn't want one more thing to clean up, to work twice as hard to fix the mistakes the higher brain makes in its attempt to help me find myself. My higher self rejoices while my lower self gets increasingly uncomfortable.

It makes sense after all; we would rather stay the same even if it is awful, just because we already know the awful, and we do not truly know how to be happy. We really do know these things, but we just do not allow ourselves to feel them. Well, you already know you are awesome, brilliant, and amazing, so just show up for yourself every day, do your best, and feel your feelings, all the while knowing that they are just feelings. If they make you happy you keep going after those. Then you keep on building them up, and your brain will start to look for those opportunities regularly. This is happiness.

As the saying goes, it is not what happens to us, it is how we interpret what happens to us that is the magic. One of my older siblings once said to me, "When you have a challenge, rather than seeing it in its hardship form, why don't you immediately say 'Thank you,' and see what you can learn from the circumstance." Two things happen here: first, you will definitely be happier because your body will quickly get into rest-and-digest mode and your breathing will regulate itself; and second, you will be a solution to the challenge you are currently facing, because rather than going into crisis mode, you will be going into repair mode, which means you will try to become a positive influence on a negative situation. Try it next time you have a challenge; this was a game changer for me in my life.

Whoever hurt you, whether it was your family, society, or yourself, you must stop the habit of doing it to yourself. You have to say: *Hey, all of you stop, get out, and get away from me. I am going to take good care of myself, I am going to meditate and find out who I am, what I like, and how I can live the best life in this journey.* Depending on where you are in your journey of self-love and self-discovery, you could also just take the time to cultivate the connection with yourself. You may think that external powers run your life, but eventually you will get to the point where you understand this is not true and it will never be true. Once you get to these levels of being, you will feel happier and more content, so it is important to do the meditation breath work to help you get to those levels of understanding.

Meditation does not have to be a certain way, just your way. I have said this several times, and it bears repeating. It is healthy for you to be you, however you are, without any excuses to yourself and others. Remember, though: when you meet yourself and you are loving, gentle, and kind, you will see yourself more clearly.

Sometimes, we are given mixed messages in movies, books, ideas, or traditions. We are told that we should not be selfish. There is no judgment here, there are only different people, groups, and societies that live life in different manners. The bottom line is that there is not one right way to live, but your happiness is the ultimate marker if you are living your truth and are connected to yourself.

You can be happy now on the life journey you are traveling on. It is not about enjoying the journey *or* the destination, but enjoying the journey *and* the destination. The difference is that you want to be happy now; if you are not, then you must adjust your life until you make it happen. Again, I am not talking about a happiness that your neighbor, your cousin, your friend, your sister's friends, or anyone else has. When you meditate and you find out what your happiness truly is, that is what you will work toward, and that is where you want to be, because that will make you intrinsically and fully happy.

> *It is not about enjoying the journey or the destination, but enjoying the journey and the destination.*

We can never really get a solution by listening to the outside noise. I found a website back in 2014, around the time when I was looking for a therapist after I had my major skiing injury. On the website there was a little story about a person who had lost the key to their house and had gone to look for it outside in their yard. Then some neighbors saw they were looking for something and said, "What are you looking for?" The person replied that they were looking for the key to their home, and when the neighbor asked, "Where did you see it last?" they responded with, "Inside the house."

The moral of this story is that the key the person was looking for was inside their house all along, if only they'd thought to check there. Similarly, if you are looking for answers outside of yourself, but all the answers are within you, then you should look inside yourself. Doesn't that sound so simple, yet so counterintuitive? If I already have all the answers I need, then why do I have to go pay a therapist to help me gain access to them? Because sometimes we do not know how to access them, and meditation is giving you the key to your house and helping you find your happiness.

If we have been raised by people, communities, and dogmas that tell us we are clueless, that we have no idea what is happening at any time, or that we are not wise enough to learn, then we just take it as gospel truth. We think, *Great, I do not have to think, I do not have to waste my time on anything that is outside of my scope of understanding, I do not have to work to try to figure out how to make myself happy, because the outer world will do that.* This is the challenge that we face when we look at the external world to make us happy and we do not take the time to find out who we are inside and what we need.

I can see why some external influences would like you to just go with the flow, and I do think there is a time and a place for this. I especially think this is the way to do it when you have an amazing relationship with yourself. When you have that, you know yourself and can enjoy yourself with others and the world. And you never have to get into a whole enlightenment state, or a "woo-woo" state of mind that makes no sense to you. Instead, always, and at every point, you must be there for yourself with gentleness, self-love, self-care, and happiness. True happiness, all-encompassing happiness, to live a wonderful life.

It is important to remember that simply because you live in happiness does not mean that you will not have to deal with life. It is not about not having challenges, but it is more about how we interpret what is happening to us in our life.

If we look at the challenges we face from a meditation mindset, what we have to go through becomes easier for us to bear, and we don't put more worry, fear, or hardship on an already challenging time. Saying "thank you" changes everything. It allows you to deal with life from a more peaceful stance. When I first used this strategy, it allowed me to back off the challenge and gently take in what had happened. I was able to accept what had happened, and most importantly it allowed me to show up in a more mature and respectful manner. I liked myself dealing with this hardship with a clear mind. I immediately started the healing and recovery cycle, which is what everyone needs when challenges arise in our lives.

> *It is not about not having challenges, but it is more about how we interpret what is happening to us in our life.*

You can be happy all the time. You can be happy even when it seems impossible, because it comes from your frame of mind, from your self-knowledge, from you knowing that it does not matter what happens, you will always be okay, you will always be loved unconditionally, and you will always be gentle with yourself. The truth is no one can ever take these things away from you; your home is your heart, your home is your happiness. Everything else is transitory, but your unconditional self-love is constant, your happiness is constant. This is your superpower.

MEDITATION

BREATHE IN AND OUT softly, then repeat the following:

"It is safe for me to be happy, healthy, successful, and satisfied.

"Happiness is easy for me to have, and I enjoy my days always.

"It is safe for me to be happy, healthy, successful, and satisfied.

"Happiness is all around me, and I love to be happy.

"It is safe for me to enjoy myself, and to nurture my heart's desire, I am truly grateful for my happy life.

"It is safe for me to be happy, healthy, successful, and satisfied."

Let all the words and affirmations run through your whole body, feel the words in every cell, help your body, mind, and soul transform into the unconditional self-love these words hold for you. Let the words permeate and stay with you.

Hold onto these feelings throughout the day. Do your breath work with these affirmations regularly in order to build the neural pathway in your brain. Your brain will automatically start looking for situations, people, and places that will make you happy. It will become a positive habit you can cultivate.

QUESTIONS

- Is there a voice in your head that says long-term meditation is unattainable?
- What makes you truly happy?
- Are you enjoying your journey, or are you just hoping to reach a destination or milestone?

10
YOUR JOURNEY

"How do you experience personal freedom, a life absent from daily fear, worry, or anxiety? Is it really possible to live an incredible life? I say yes, it is possible. No matter your age or personal history, it is never too late to choose to create an incredible life . . . This journey is not for the faint-hearted. As you travel, think short sprints, then rest and rejuvenate. To help you succeed, get your checklist in order. It is essential to set the framework and pack the right supplies to help strengthen your commitment to change even when you get stuck . . . Determine your core values. When your values are clear, your decisions are easy, because your values act like a compass for decision making."

—Kim Crumpler, *From Fear to Freedom*[31]

I traveled to Italy for my fortieth birthday, and that same year my mother turned eighty, so we celebrated together. My mother had me when she was forty, so we always had our big birthdays together. When I turned ten, she turned fifty, when I turned thirty, she turned sixty, and so on and so forth.

My mother told me that she could not believe she was taking such an amazing vacation with me, going to the

Vatican. We were actually on a cruise, which we boarded in Spain, so we flew there so we could travel to a couple of other countries in Europe. I wanted to go to the Vatican to see Michaelangelo's famous ceiling in the Sistine Chapel. This was my goal for my fortieth birthday, and we made it happen. It was an hour's drive to the Vatican from where the cruise boarded.

While at the Vatican, when I saw the ceiling, I could literally imagine Michaelangelo painting in there with us, and I felt humbled by the experience. After all this time, it still warms my heart to think that I was able to experience this with my mother, too. Love you, Mom!

This is just one experience that has enriched my life. I have also learned so many lessons from growing up in a home with so many siblings. I was bound to learn a thing or two that would help me in my life. I did have fun climbing trees and being an acrobat when I was in grade school, and I learned how to be patient and respectful. I learned how to stand up for myself and call on my courage when I needed it.

In our home growing up, I would eat cherries from our cherry tree and pomegranates from our pomegranate tree. I especially remember having pecans when I would walk home after school and sports practice; there was nothing as delicious and tasty as a pecan after a long day and a great workout. I remember it was a lot of work getting to the meat of the pecan, but it sure was good once you got there. I would walk for miles and just enjoy the beautiful open air, the peace and calm. That happiness is what I aspire to get back to every time I do breath work. My journey has been beautiful, and the meditation is just making my journey more enjoyable every day.

We all intrinsically know what we need on our life journey. To listen to that voice inside your head is the biggest gift you can give yourself. Meditate to reach your dreams. Just as I had a dream to go to the Vatican to see Michaelangelo's beautiful ceiling, so too can you do whatever you want on your journey in this life. Doing breath work can not only help you get there, but it can give you the space to see what it is that your heart wants and needs.

As I mentioned before, when I was in my late twenties, I lost my grandfather, my youngest brother, and my long-term relationship. I was completely devasted, sad, and depressed. It was a very hard time for me; I was torn apart from the inside out. My mother wanted me to come back home and live with her, because she was worried about me. I already touched on this part of the story earlier, but there is another piece that I would like to share with you.

The detail I skipped is that my mother told me when she talked to me that if I was determined not to go home, then I at least should promise to see a priest. My mother liked to read the Bible and pray, and it made sense that she would feel better if I did this as an alternative to going back home. So that week on Sunday, after I had talked to her and agreed that I would do this to help her feel better, I found a Catholic church. I did not go in for the sermon, but I did meet with the priest when everyone was leaving; I waited until there was no one there at the door with the priest and then I mustered up the courage to go and speak to him. I told him I was there because my mother told me to be.

I think the priest was a bit confused, and I cannot recall if I gave him a backstory or not. I just remember I was very nervous, and I was a little angry that as an adult, graduated from college with a great job, I was still listening to my mom as if I were a child. I know my mom had her heart in the right place, but it was just strange for me, and I felt uncomfortable.

The beauty unfolded right in front of me during our conversation. After listening to me, he looked me in the eyes and spoke to me in a very nice and gentle tone. The priest said, "First, do not listen to your mother, and second, you have all the answers." He knew I had to listen to myself and what I needed in order to heal from my very large losses at home.

This is why my mother thought that I needed to talk to someone to help me with the healing process. In my mother's life, because she was Catholic, this is where she found comfort. Since she knew I was not going to read the Bible, she thought at least I could talk to someone that she trusted through her Catholic faith.

I would have to figure out how to soothe, heal, and get through these tough times away from her. I would be doing the healing where I was at, on my own, without the direct help and love of my mother. I knew this was hard for her and it was hard for me, but I needed to do this for my own personal growth.

YOUR JOURNEY

My mom was right; the priest did in fact help me, and the message gave me some clarity. It was exactly what I needed to hear in that moment: to recognize that I was in some serious emotional pain, but I was going to be okay. I was going to make it out of the sadness, the depression, and the pain of all the loss I had just gone through.

I felt worlds better, because I knew there was light at the end of the tunnel. Would I be able to bear all this pain, loss, and sorrow? Would I be able to bear all this weight, my tears, and my lethargy? It was real, it was debilitating, and it sucked. I hated feeling so damn sad, so lost and confused.

I had felt sad and confused in the past, but this was completely different; this was as if the whole ocean was sitting on my chest, like I was drowning under the weight of my pain and loss. I hated it, and I just wanted it all to go away. My mother was concerned about me because I did not have a lot of tolerance for pain; remember, most of my life I kept myself so busy I did not have the space to feel. It was easier that way: be so busy you will think you are okay.

SOMETIMES WE ARE given information that makes us try to live impossible lives; we are supposed to give all of ourselves over to others, but why? Even on a plane everyone knows you give yourself the oxygen before you can help anyone else. We seek to be the best selves we can be, so at any other point in our lives we balk at the idea of saving ourselves first. Why are meditation and self-care so difficult to accept into our lives? Why do we have to explain to everyone what we are doing and care so much about their approval?

I have had so much help in my life; some from professionals and even more from kind souls who just want to offer their help. I truly love the kind souls, we all do, and you are one of them, just waiting to blossom. A gentle reminder: fake-it-till-you-make-it will not work here. As a matter of fact, faking it will actively prevent you from getting in touch with yourself and your feelings. And I'm not talking about the fake-it-till-you-make-it you tap into to find the courage to go beyond your comfort zone. You must be honest with yourself while meditating to find your home, your happiness, and your unconditional self-love. There is nothing else quite so powerful.

That said, you have your superpowers, they are yours, and no one can take them from you. Can you believe that you cannot take them from yourself, either? It is like the universe; things are growing and changing constantly.

In terms of your own body, the cells are constantly being replenished by new cells. This is all being done automatically, and there are systems working out there whether we are aware of them or not. Your happiness is within you; it is working all the time. It is never going away, and you cannot make it go away. You must focus on it gently at first, because it may feel a little weird to think about, but that happiness is always there. We get off-track, and then we get lost; this is how we lose ourselves. We get lost because we think our homes are somehow external from us, but they are not.

Your home is self-love, unconditional self-love. The gentleness, the care, the fun, the excitement, the smile, the happiness—they are always already there, along with the happiness that lets you know you are awesome, you are amazing, you are wonderful, and you are loved: the unconditional self-love that brings you everything you've ever dreamed of. It has always been present in you. I have mixed feelings, because as I think about the unlimited stores of happiness in our bodies, I also think about how much the people in my life would benefit from discovering it; they could be genuinely content and successful in the state they are today, every day.

I know I make it sound as if this stuff is so easy and everyone can do it at any point. If you pick up your breathing meditation practice, yes, for sure, you will reach this point. You will be operating on all cylinders, which means you will be walking around with confidence, abundance, love, and lots and lots of strength and power—all good energy.

You will be all lit up like a Christmas tree, and it will come from your soul. You will not care to compare, judge, or be harsh because you will have built a beautiful practice of meditation. You will be more self-aware and self-knowing, which is so much more attractive than anything else in this world. All you have to do is give yourself permission to shed your misconceptions and doubts and start meditation.

It sounds so weird, doesn't it? *Give myself permission? Am I a child?* We are so uncomfortable with failure, but the sister of that is success. We are afraid both of failure and success; go figure. We know our lower self would be happier just staying put. If it ain't broke, don't fix it, right? Why change now? Why try something new?

Well, you are reading this meditation book because you want to find out how meditation can help you. There is a part of you that is moving you forward and is seeking more of your truth, more of your happiness. It wants to continue its journey. I say, good for you! Celebrate, because you are the risk-taker. Even if the risk-taking is in bite sizes, it moves you forward all the same. Bite-size growth is the best way to do it, because it is the only way that lasts. You are the only expert on what you need, and trust me, you will feel great having this expertise.

Others will welcome your awesomeness as you begin to have unconditional self-love; they will see how wonderful and beautiful your relationship with yourself is, and they will also want to grow to know themselves, to find their happiness and true bliss.

As Marianne Williamson said: "Our deepest fear is not that we are inadequate. Our deepest fear is that we are powerful beyond measure." When you can find your light and inner beauty and let it shine, you give others the confidence to do it as well.[32] We are often part of a system, and we think if we stray from the norm it may screw things up for everyone else; that could not be further from the truth. I know we feel that we have a lot of influence and power over others, but we have less than we think. We mostly only have power over ourselves, and even then, we do not truly know ourselves enough to revel in our own beauty, love, power, and strength.

Sometimes we get confused or disappointed that we do not understand life or cannot make sense of our environment. Then we go to the external world, and this is where we start to find fault in our home and happiness. First, we start to take inventory of our environment; we begin to look at ourselves and start to compare ourselves to others, then we start to abandon ourselves because we think that we must become like others: look like them, act like them, literally be them. Where the heck did this come from? Why would we do this to ourselves?

Just as the seed grows into something spectacularly bigger than itself, just as your cells are magically replaced with new cells on a regular basis, we also are developing. We get these urges, these needs, both biological and emotional, but what ends up happening is that we begin to abandon ourselves. And here is where the hero's journey commences.

What is your hero's journey? Life is full of setbacks and surges forward, but the steps back seem more impactful. You see, just when things were starting to get good, you decided that you would abandon yourself; we think others

Life is full of setbacks and surges forward, but the steps back seem more impactful.

abandon us, but no one can ever abandon us, because we are the real creators of the world. This is our world, so if we think that someone is doing something so impactful to us that it is changing our reality, then we are not in alignment with our true selves. It is when we get reconnected with our true selves that we can start to grow again; we can start to find our home and our happiness. It is so wonderful, this thing we call life, and your journey is also wonderful; somebody lied to us and told us we were boring, a dud, and our journeys sucked. Maybe they are one of the people who are faking it. But we don't begrudge them, because they are trying their best, just as we are trying our best. This is the beauty of meditation; you find yourself, so you see everyone else in their lanes and on their journeys, and you can enjoy that. You are in happiness and in your home, and you will never be lost again, because you found the key. Sure, life will happen, but you will enjoy both the ebbs and flows of life.

Meditating will help you get rid of perfectionism. When I learned how to meditate, I did not think of perfectionism so much; I realized I would mostly think about it if I got tired, if I was not giving myself self-care, if I was pushing myself too hard. The truth is, there is a difference between just being passionate or showing up, and putting all your heart into it, because when you are done, you feel amazing. You do not worry about the results, because you were present, you were there, and you brought all of yourself; you did not leave half of yourself at home. What was important was the journey, not the destination.

YOUR JOURNEY

YOU ARE UNIQUE; nobody can tell you who you are but you. When people are telling you who you are, they are putting you in a little box. I remember doing some work once on personal growth, and part of what I was learning was not to succumb to people giving you either positive kudos or negative criticism.

The idea is that both are from the same vein, and that both comments are telling you what you *should* be happy or unhappy about. The reality is that you can be however you want to be, whenever you want to be. If you need something, then it is your job to take good care of yourself and get what you need; don't wait for someone else to do it for you.

When you think about it, do the people that are praising you or knocking you down really know who you are? We share similarities with all humans, but you are still unique in how you feel, what you need, and what will make your soul happy. Remember, I am always talking about true happiness, learned through meditation and powerful personal growth work. One way personal growth is "achieved" is through the fake-it-till-you-make-it strategy, and the other is a difficult and deep journey to determine how you will show up for yourself.

Trust me, if you do the work, all the confusion just starts to slide off, and it is so gentle that you do not even call it confusion; you call it something that is not true to you, something that is not in alignment with your true self, with your soul, with your inner knowing. No one will have anything negative to say about it, because meeting yourself is so gentle that your whole world will start to say yes to you. The whole world will praise you for taking the time to take care of yourself, for finding and loving yourself. This is what it means to find true internal happiness, this is what it means to truly live.

What is true internal happiness? I have been doing personal work for such a long time, and what it means, essentially, is to care about yourself. What I love about it is that you can revel in your beauty wherever you are. You can completely and utterly love yourself, and you can turn your attention away from anyone who thinks otherwise.

As I write this, I am almost in disbelief. My lower brain is saying, *But what if you need me to be in fight or flight all the time?* I love my survival self because it has helped me develop "Spidey senses" when I was just trying to figure out my world, but I always knew that there was more.

When you start to truly get connected with your internal self and begin to know exactly what you need, all of these characters hurting you and the negative circumstances conspiring against you start to disappear. The reason is that when you begin to meditate and begin to truly listen to yourself, you gently move away from anything that can hurt you, anything that causes you harm. It seems unrealistic, but it is totally not. You end up going down a different road.

I knew when I saw gentle, loving, caring, and kind people around me that it was possible to live that way. When I saw these people living their best lives, I knew there was a place where all of that happiness was waiting for me, and it was already within me. People would reach out a hand to me and want to give me love; I was always so confused but also grateful for these people.

This is what I find amazing: no matter who we are and no matter where we come from, we all know that these people exist all around the world and that they have something very special that is in each one of us. We also know that we can have it and it is always ready for us to take, but most of us live our lives through our lower brain. I do not think we do this because we choose to; I think we do this because it is a long journey to understand how to get to the other side to our home, our happiness. Two points here: your home is you, and you are your home.

Your home is you, and you are your home.

The heart has tons of neurons, and they go all over your body. There are more neurons and information receptors sent from your heart than your brain. I want to point out that there is such a thing as a gate built around your heart. When people are hurt or traumatized, they will build a wall in order to protect themselves, for their survival. With a meditation practice, you can start to bring down that structure surrounding your heart.

Why would anyone care to do this? Sure, by locking away your heart you do not get hurt. However, you are not allowing yourself to feel happiness, either. I know it seems unfair, but it makes a lot of sense when you stop and think about it.

We should give some thought to the way we feel. If we are happy we are home, we feel great, the world looks lovely. But if we do not feel well, we are fearful or afraid. We are sad, depressed, and feel unwell. That is not your home. Your home is in happiness; when you were born, even if you were colicky or whatever else, you were still happy.

Happiness then is your home, even if you don't believe it fully just yet. Your home is happiness. It is a laughably simple concept; it is simple as I write it, and it is simple as I think about it, so what is the problem? There is no problem here; do not construct unnecessary obstacles. Your job is to be happy, healthy, and successful, and I know you've got this!

Even if your lower self is saying, *No way, no way, this is all so unrealistic; this person does not know what they are saying*, recognize that there is also that voice in all of us, our advocate, that says, *It is about time! I am ready to go home; I am ready to be truly happy. I am ready to do the work. I am ready to love myself. I am ready to take good care of myself. I am ready to be there for myself. I am ready to be gentle with myself.*

THERE IS ANOTHER REASON that I did not pick up meditation as a regular practice for a time. I did not understand how easy it was to do; I did not understand the benefits that I would get from meditating. This means that I did not meditate long enough for it to become a habit.

Habits, as we have talked about earlier, are another

YOUR JOURNEY

piece of the puzzle. I know that this is supposed to be a simple book on meditating, but as I write this book, I am reminded of all the self-help books I have read. I am trying to convey the importance of the practice of meditating so that you may improve your life.

When I was out of college, I was looking into yoga to help keep me happy and healthy because it was something I was familiar with. I truly loved the meditation, and I wanted to continue to grow in it. I would do a yoga class, and we would do exercises along with some meditation sprinkled throughout. What I found was that if the instructor was happy and in alignment with themselves, meaning they did the work to find their home or their happy place, I felt extremely good, and I usually benefited tremendously from the class. But if the instructor was not practicing what they were teaching, then those classes were almost more stressful than the real life problems I was trying to escape.

That was my journey with yoga and trying to create a meditation practice, and I did not have much luck. Learning all the different names of the poses and trying to do them, as well as keeping up with the classes, was also more stress than it was worth for me.

These days, I am doing meditational running, which feels good in so many ways. It is a slow jog while listening to some meditation sounds, and I simply get in the flow. When doing things like this you are moving your body, so you get to have a whole mind-body experience where you feel completely relaxed and all your worries, questions, and anything else that may be in your brain get turned off for the time it takes you to finish your very short, yet powerful meditation run.

You can meditate anywhere while doing something you love, and you should do it because it helps you find yourself. It helps you find your way home. It would be as if you were telling yourself a narrative. You see, when we criticize, judge, get angry, or hate others, we are not really pushing those feelings onto them, *we* are feeling them. This is your world, this is your home, this is your life. Nothing exists that you do not create first in your mind, in your life. How is this possible? No one exists but you; no one influences you but you; no one controls you but you.

No one exists but you; no one influences you but you; no one controls you but you.

Think about the feelings you experience. You are happy. You are sad. You are depressed. You are exhilarated. You are beyond laughter. You are on top of the world. You are going to crawl into a hole. You are going to jump for joy. You are going to hide in a closet. You are going to yell from a rooftop how happy you are.

What thread do you see in all of these? The presence of you.

YES, YOU. The word YOU! YOU! YOU!

You are you, and you will always be you, and I hope you learn how to celebrate you, not from a superficial level, but from a gentle, knowing, and loving place.

YOUR JOURNEY

I take my happiness and my self-love very seriously, and I am gentle and caring with myself always. This is where you want to be. The world will do what the world will do; you will be happy when you decide to take the time out to take good care of yourself. It is not that hard, and you can start with meditation.

Always remember: meditation is free, you can do it anywhere, and you can get your lower brain to jump on board and see that this meditation stuff has absolutely no negative side effects at all. It is the most gentle and loving way you can start connecting your lower brain to your higher brain, your head to your body.

Many of us are walking around disconnected because we do not know any better, but when we figure it out, we should make the necessary changes. It goes back to the idea that every single one of us is doing our best, every single one of us deserves love, care, and gentleness: every single one of us—every single one of us.

One last time: every single one of us deserves love, care, and gentleness.

Remember, you are the only one that exists in this world; no one else exists but you, so before you let your lower brain think about how that's not true, remind yourself that you deserve love, care, and gentleness.

Every single one of us deserves love, care, and gentleness.

The world and the universe will take care of the rest. Your job is to be happy. Again, I will continue to say that happiness is homecoming, a return to your true self that knows that it needs self-love, self-care, and tons and tons of kindness and warmth. You need this, I need this, we all need to give this to ourselves, always.

The blueprint is within you. It has been within you all along.

YOU CAN MEDITATE as little or as much as you want to. This is not one size fits all, so first and foremost, learn the benefits of meditation. Meditation is not for the faint of heart. Meditation will transform your life immediately. Meditation is not easy, but it is worth it.

I like to see that what I am doing is going to make a difference in the quality of my life, and if my job is to be happy, healthy, and successful, then for me to keep myself strong and healthy physically is part of my self-care. You can do anything to ensure that you are taking care of yourself physically—walking, yoga, stretching, anything to keep you moving. There are whole other books on the benefits of exercising and movement on mental and physical wellbeing. Also, remember it is up to you. You are the one who gets to decide, no one else, so do not think that you must do what your friend, your aunt, or uncle, or your senator are doing.

Listening to yourself, your body, and your energy levels are extremely important. You must take the time to listen to yourself to know what you need to do next. I'm not saying that taking the time to listen to myself is going to be a long, drawn-out story, that it is going to take me forever to figure it out, or that I must go to some mountain top and try to figure out my entire life right away. Again, you do not need the perfect place.

It's a little dramatic, but people really think this way. I thought, *How do those people do it? How do they know exactly how to be happy?* I wondered if either they had the perfect conditions to figure out their true selves, or they were born with perfect happiness. Somehow, though, I knew this was not true.

Deep down inside, I knew that it was much easier to get access to happiness. I still did not have the answers, and I was so used to being so busy that I did not want to take the time to understand, or I was too afraid to take the time to understand in order to learn and grow.

When we think of our own truth, we can only think in terms of what we know. There is a difference between thinking and feeling. In our society, we tend to have a group that thinks we should make decisions from our intellectual minds (and this is still prevalent today), and to a large extent this is completely logical.

Emotional intelligence, or EI, is the study of intelligence from the heart or from your emotions. Science wanted nothing to do with emotions, as they did not fit in the sphere of science, and now they are finding out that emotions and the heart are powerful indicators of many advances in the human journey.

By meditating, we can start to see what is truly going on inside of us. Again, it takes time for us to build trust with ourselves. All good things take time, and they are worth it if they are sustainable. We can make decisions not only with our minds, but with our emotions as well.

We can become confident in showing up for ourselves so that we can finally see what we truly need. As I have said before, no one will argue with this. If anything, people will automatically know that you are showing up completely, and no one disrespects that.

COULD MEDITATION HELP you deal with growth, new opportunities? For example, new jobs, relationships that you may have thought could be fun, or stressful situations—more stressful than you think you can handle? Yes, learning and picking up a meditation practice can help you with this. It is realistic for you to learn, grow, and be ready to move again from one challenge to the next in a steady, confident state. When you meditate, you can answer many of your questions and concerns, and this can help you find clarity and confidence.

If there is anything you have absorbed from this book, it is that your mind is your happiness, and what you let into your mind, whether it is making you happy or not, is your choice. You can choose if you are happy or not, you can choose what to put into your mind, you can choose how you want to spend your time, and most importantly, you can choose how to take care of yourself with unconditional self-love.

Why would we want to literally waste our time with

what is not making us happy? Truly, we are wasting our time. Sometimes I feel that I must be blunt with myself, but then I must backtrack and think whether it is helpful. Is it gentle? Am I being abrasive with myself? If I am being abrasive with myself, why am I doing this?

There is no real difference in outcome when you are working on something in the way you get yourself to do something. The only real difference is in the way it makes you feel. Are you feeling happy? Are you feeling neutral? Are you feeling stressed? These are a lot of questions, but they will help you start to unravel how you are talking to yourself. They will allow you to decide to talk to yourself in a way that is gentle, that makes you happy and able to get your tasks done and enjoy your life. Here is an example of a dialogue in your head that you may not even be aware of:

> Me to Self: I must be abrasive with myself so we can get stuff done; otherwise we will not get anything done.

> Mind of Unconditional Self-Love: No, you do not have to be abrasive with yourself. There are other ways to speak to yourself to get things done, and that is with a gentle, loving voice.

> Me to Self: No, I must be abrasive, as this is the only way I will do anything. Otherwise, I will just not get what I need to get done completed.

Mind of Unconditional Self-Love: There are many ways to get things done. Abrasive is one way, but it probably does not make you feel good. You can also talk to yourself in a loving, gentle, and caring way. You are still conveying the same message, plus you are filling yourself up with care and love. Being kind makes you feel so much better; it makes you feel the love for yourself, and it makes your heart smile. It doesn't take any more effort than being harsh, but the benefits are endless. You will feel good and loved. You can be kind, loving, and caring to yourself and also get everything done that you wanted to get done from your calmer, happier self.

This is a great example of how self-talk can work. We do not stop to think about the process of our internal dialogue—however, it is important to consider and sometimes even necessary. We do not even realize we are talking to ourselves this way, and it can have unconscious consequences.

We feel our feelings, but we never take the time to connect them to our minds and bodies. When we allow ourselves to stress out, we feel upset. Many times, we get flustered or frustrated. The sad thing is that we learned this somewhere outside of ourselves and we don't even realize it.

What this means is that the voices that we use to speak to ourselves are not from us. When we were little kids learning how to walk and we fell down, we did not say, *Hey, what's wrong with you?* or *What the heck are you thinking? Why can't you walk?* No, we fell down, laughed, cried, or experienced whatever emotion we had, got over it, and then tried again until we learned how to walk. The voice from above is not the voice that says, *No problem, let's just keep at it and we will get there.*

How do you get your voice back? As we have seen, we have to give ourselves time to find out what we need: not our neighbor, not our sister, not our father, not our great-great uncle Ben or his brother Jerry. We want to find our voice. We can pretend that we really do not care; if you are okay with the way you talk to yourself, then you can move on and go find another great book to read and grow in a different way. However, if you would like to find out how to find your true bliss through meditation, giving it a go is the next step.

Remember, I mentioned earlier that there are a lot of ways to meditate, so what one person may need could be completely different than what someone else may need. It is all unique to you. I hope that if you learn anything here, it is that you matter and you deserve to be super happy, healthy, successful, and living an amazing life. I hope that meditation helps you find your beauty and the gentle, loving voice we all already have available to us. We simply need to meditate to access it.

Meditating to feel better might be good enough for you for the next one to five years; if this is your goal, you're in luck, because you are the reason I am writing this book.

Self-awareness is a large part of the work I do, and let me tell you, it is not a walk in the park. If anything, it is the hardest thing I have ever had to do in my life. The reason it is so difficult is because you must study yourself. You must learn about yourself. I know that some of us pretend we know ourselves, but we are so influenced by the outside world that we do not even know who we really are, what we truly want, or what would make us completely happy.

I think sometimes when we are young and just learning, it is good to be reminded that there is not one way to get things done. We grow up around many people who love us, who are trying to help us the best way they know how. Some of us are lucky to stay on course and not disconnect from ourselves, and this is great because these people are usually the role models for others on how to get reconnected.

When we learn how to connect to ourselves and find our voice, then this automatically helps us become teachers. The reason is because when you love yourself, you are home, and you can help others find their home within themselves.

You are happy, and you can go out and live your life on your terms for the entirety of your existence. Since you have this gift, even if you do not go out and teach people with intention, you are still teaching the world by example. This means that you are an example of home, you are an example of love, caring, and gentleness. As each one of us finds our happiness, we are home, we are happy, and we are fulfilled.

Again, this is not a wonky idea that suddenly makes everything rainbows and unicorns, but rather it is about waking up to oneself. It shows us that the world exists through our lens; you are the only one who exists, and you make the choice every single day to be healthy, happy, and successful. Now it is your world, and you have arrived home.

I know what you're thinking: *But how about this, how about that, and that other thing?* Nothing else changes; the only thing that changes is your perspective. The only thing that changes is your view of the world. And now, rather than you thinking that the world is simply happening to you and you have no control over it, you can see that you are happening to the world, and you always have control of your mood, your happiness, the type of work you do, and how you live your life. And if that is your next step in your happiness and journey, you will know.

You see, when you meditate, you will find all your answers. As I said, it is all subjective and unique to each person. Even though the external world is not going to change, your internal world will change dramatically. And this in turn is what causes your outer world to change; this is what helps you reach your true happiness, your true bliss, your nirvana in this world, here and now.

And meditation is free. There are no downsides. This book is merely serving as a reminder to yourself to get out there and start your practice. As you take your journey of meditation, you will find that everything you are looking for is already here.

MEDITATION

NOW IT IS YOUR TURN. This is your journey. How will you incorporate the breathing meditation you learned?

If you ever feel intimidated or unsure about "MEDITATION," you can always pull it out and hold it in the palm of your hand to get re-acquainted with it. Now that it is your practice and you are the driver of how you want to use it, the choice is yours, always.

Remember to keep a curious mindset and continue to learn and grow.

Your breathing is always with you, and having a sense of gratitude for your breath is also a type of meditation.

Any positive attention you give to your breath speaks volumes to the rest of your body. Your body will thank you for giving your breath the proper respect it deserves.

Meditation will help you realize and fullfill your talents and potential, and it will give you the energy to enjoy your journey in a profound way.

QUESTIONS

- How have your struggles contributed to who you are as a person today?
- Do you feel at home in your own body, in your own mind?
- What is your personal goal for your meditation journey?

CONCLUSION

So what did we learn from this? How does meditation help your body?

When you do the breathing work of meditation, it encourages your body to relax. Your whole system works better. If our minds are stressed out, it can affect our entire being.

Remember that when you produce too much cortisol from being in fight-or-flight mode all day long, it also affects your body. It appears to affect some of your vital organs as well. From personal experience, I know that when I meditate, I am in better touch with what is going on with my body. It's important to create that relationship with your breath. You will feel so much better.

On busy days where you have a lot of fun stuff to do with your family and you feel exhausted, take some time off to do some meditation breathing and rest to take stock of yourself. Without crucial moments like this, you will continue to push yourself without resting. Every once in a while it's fine, but the problem starts when we make it a habit to not take breaks, which cultivates unhealthy habits and leads to breakdowns. Breathing will allow you to stop and breathe; doing this simple practice for even a minute a day will get you started on your discovery of, and ultimately a relationship with, your breath.

Meditation gives me the space to pause. If I were not doing meditation, I would constantly be looking for the next thing. Let's keep the party going! However, this only makes me tired, makes me cranky, and I almost become a different person.

You see, if we are not listening to our bodies, then our bodies will continue to go and move, but at some point, our whole system will say, *That's it, I am done. I am moving on.* This will usually be coming from an overly tired state, a state of fight or flight, because your system now has been compromised.

This happens when you've pushed yourself too far without giving yourself a break. When I was a kid this would happen to me, and I would get so tired that the only way for me to get relief was to yell, scream, bite, and kick. I literally had to get that physical sometimes. My mother tried her best to give me the space to decompress, but I was one of the youngest kids, and no one really helped me regulate my emotions in a safe and gentle manner. It's important to learn these things as an adult.

If you take nothing else from this book, remember that breathing is a great gateway into learning all the benefits that meditating can offer. Your re-connection to your soul is the goal. There are so many benefits to picking up a

CONCLUSION

meditation practice. What is truly spectacular about meditating is that we are all already breathing. Yes: breath, breathing—we do it every second of every day.

When we breathe we are alive. And when we choose to pay a little attention to breathing we are meditating. It is that easy.

It helps us be in the present. When we are in the present, our body goes into rest-and-digest. We then can relax and give every bit of our body, mind, and soul a break. Everyone needs a break; it is the kind thing to do for ourselves. Meditation helps us learn how to break habits that do not serve us anymore, that have outlived their purpose and are now simply causing us undue stress. Your health is truly worth it, and it is in your hands. Meditating is easy, free, and yours for the taking.

Your re-connection to your soul is the goal.

ACKNOWLEDGMENTS

I would like to acknowledge my husband, Aaron, and my two children, Katalia and Gabriella, for all the love and support you always give me and for all your smiles which always warm my heart. I would like to thank my mother Carmen F. Garcia for all the love and support you gave me, and for doing your best to raise sixteen children. I want to thank Carmelita Andia, Kimberly Peterson, Dr. Cheyenne Bryant, Lynn Larkin, Sarah Schneider, Sarah McCarthy, Lauren Shea, and Gabriella Condi for all the beautiful thank-you cards you always send me. I want to thank all my sports, life, and executive coaches; you have all touched my life and have helped me become a better person.

Thank you to Amber Vilhauer at NGNG for all your help and for introducing me to Whitney Gossett and the team at Content Capital, who are absolutely amazing. Lauren Hall and Nayla Zylberberg, thank you so much for all your help and amazing talent with the book.

I would love to thank all the self-help book gurus out there for sharing your stories and helping us out, and helping us learn how to live happier, more fulfilled lives. I am eternally grateful for the light and love you have poured into your books. Thank you, thank you, thank you. I especially want to thank the readers for allowing me to share my stories, meditation, and breathing work with you. May your lives be happy, healthy, full of love, beauty, success, and lots and lots of unconditional love, from yourself and others.

ENDNOTES

Introduction

1 Ravikant, Kamal. *Love Yourself Like Your Life Depends on It,* Perseus Design, USA. Pg. 18.
2 Chatterjee, Dr. Rangan. *How to Make Disease Disappear,* Harper Collins Paperback Edition, 2019, USA. Pg. 42.
3 Ibid.

Chapter One: My Journey

4 Childre, Doc and Howard Martin, with Donna Beech. *The Heartmath Solution,* Harper Collins Publishers, Paperback Edition, 2000, New York. Page 99.
5 Hansen, Kathryn. *Brain over Binge.* Camellia Publishing, 2011, Columbus, GA.
6 Dweck, Carol S. *Mindset: The New Psychology of Success,* Random House, 2006, New York.
7 Levinson, Jay Conrad. *Guerilla Marketing: Secrets for Making Big Profits from Your Small Business,* Houghton Mifflin, 1984, Boston, MA.

Chapter Two: Pick Your Place

8 Rangan, Dr. Chatterjee. "Your Daily Plan to Feel Great for

Life," in *Feel Better in 5,* BenBella Books, 2020, USA. Pg. 92.

Chapter Three: Method

9 Hof, Wim. "Activate Your Full Human Potential," in *The Wim Hof Method.* Sounds True, 2020, Boulder, CO. Pg. 45.
10 Mandal, Dr. Ananya. "What Is the Nervous System?" in *News-Medical Life Sciences,* Cashin-Garbutt, April, ed., https://www.news-medical.net/health/What-is-the-Nervous-System.aspx, viewed 21 January 2021.
11 Khuly, Dr. Patty. "Euthanasia: Why Some Owners Choose to Stay and Some Choose to Go," in VetStreet, 20 September 2012, http://www.vetstreet.com/our-pet-experts/euthanasia-why-some-owners-choose-to-stay-and-some-choose-to-go.

Chapter Four: Hormones

12 Pope, Alexandra and Sjanie Hugo Wurlitzer. *Wild Power,* Hay House, 2017, USA. Pp. 164–165.
13 Gottman, John. *The Seven Principles for Making Marriage Work,* Orion Publisher, 2000, London, England.
14 Robbins, Mel. *The 5 Second Rule: Transform your Life, Work, and Confidence with Everyday Courage,* Post Hill Press, 2017, USA.
15 Canfield, Jack. *Self-Esteem & Peak Performance,* Audio CD, Career Track, 1990, USA.
16 Berman, Laura. *Quantum Love: Use Your Body's Atomic Energy to Create the Relationship You Desire,* Abridged Audiobook, Hay House, 2016, USA.

ENDNOTES

Chapter Five: Rest and Digest

17 Bryant, Dr. Cheyenne. "The Power and Guidance to Implement Peace, Joy, Balance and Financial Abundance in Your Life," in *Mental Detox*, Book Baby, 2014, USA. Pg 31.
18 Hicks, Abraham. "All Diseases Are Curable." YouTube, https://www.youtube.com/watch?v=26c0eTPVEYc, viewed 21 January 2018.
19 Ross, Julia. "The 4-Step Program to Take Charge of Your Emotions-Today," in *The Mood Cure*, Penguin Life, 2003, USA, *The Diet Cure: The 8-Step Program to Rebalance Your Body Chemistry and End Food Cravings, Weight Problems, and Mood-Swings—Now*, Viking Adult, 1999, USA.

Chapter Six: Clarity

20 Rangan, Dr. Chatterjee. "Your Daily Plan to Feel Great for Life." Pg. 22.
21 Clear, James. *Atomic Habits: An Easy & Proven Way to Build Good Habits & Break Bad Ones*, Avery, 2018, USA. Chapter 5.
22 Hill, Napoleon. *Think and Grow Rich: The Landmark Bestseller Now Revised and Updated for the 21st Century* (Think and Grow Rich Series), TarcherPerigee, 2005, USA.
23 Bloomfield, Harold H. and Melba Colgrove. *How to Survive the Loss of a Love*, Prelude Press, 2006, USA.

Chapter Seven: Why Now?

24 Newman, Mildred and Bernard Berkowitz. *How to Be Your Own Best Friend*, Ballantine Books Trade Paperback Edition, 2016, USA. Pg. 48.
25 Neff, Kristin. *Self-Compassion: The Proven Power of Being Kind*

to *Yourself*, William Morrow Paperbacks, 2015, USA.

Chapter Eight: Health

26 Chatterjee, *How to Make Disease Disappear*. Pg. 42.
27 Clear, James. *Atomic Habits*.

Chapter Nine: Happiness

28 Jones, Mary. "Believe in Yourself!" in *Incredible Life*, Power Dynamics Publishing, 2010, San Francisco, CA.
29 Amara, Heather Ash. "A Simple Process to Transform Confusion Into Clarity and Pain into Peace," in *The Warrior Heart Practice*, St. Martin's Publishing Group, 2020.
30 Wieder, Marcia. *Dream: Clarify and Create What You Want*. Next Century Publishing, 2016, USA.

Chapter Ten: Your Journey

31 *Crumpler, Kim. "From Freedom To Fear, Commit to Change."* Incredible Life, Power Dynamics Publishing, 2010, USA. Pp. 163–169.
32 Grady, Constance. "Why Marianne Williamson's Most Famous Passage Keeps Getting Cited as a Nelson Mandela Quote," in *Vox*, 30 July 2019, https://www.vox.com/culture/2019/7/30/20699833/marianne-williamson-our-deepest-fear-nelson-mandela-return-to-love.

MONICA GARCIA DUGGAL is a serial entrepreneur, mom, wife, marathon runner, Ironman Triathalon superstar, migraine headache survivor, speaker, and co-founder of WholeHealthPlan.com. She holds an English and Rhetoric double major degree from UC Berkeley, and an Executive Master's in Business Administration from the University of Washington Foster School of Business. She has received Executive and business education from the NYU Stern School of Business; the University of Chicago Booth School of Business; University of Berkeley Haas School of Business; and the MIT Sloan School of Management. Monica is the founder of the Women's Executive Leadership for Mentors and Mentees, and Financing Women in Technology. Her strong background in Neuroscience for Leadership, Finance, and Self-Development have encouraged her to co-found www.WholeHealthPlan.com with her husband, which has revolutionized how individuals think about their health and overall lifestyles. Monica believes that if we choose to, we can control the thoughts we think, enabling us to create the life we want.

Monica lives in the great northwest with her husband of twenty years, two children, dog, and cat. Monica loves reading books on neuroscience, psychology, self-development, business, economics, finance, and anything that makes her laugh. She especially loves to snuggle up with a good book on a cold winter day in front of the fireplace with a nice cup of chamomile tea.

Visit the author at www.WholeHealthPlan.com.

www.ingramcontent.com/pod-product-compliance
Lightning Source LLC
Chambersburg PA
CBHW021440070526
44577CB00002B/225